LOVE

AND

FAMILY

LIFE

LOVE AND FAMILY LIFE

Swami Rama

The Himalayan International Institute
of Yoga Science and Philosophy
of the U.S.A.
Honesdale, Pennsylvania

© 1992, 1998
The Himalayan International Institute
of Yoga Science and Philosophy of the USA
RR 1, Box 400
Honesdale, PA 18431 USA

First Printing 1992, Second Printing 1998

Portions of some chapters of this book were previously published in a somewhat different form in *Marriage, Parenthood and Enlightenment* by Swami Rama.

The paper used in this publication meets the minimum requirements of the American National Standard for Information Sciences—Permanence of Paper for Printed Library Materials, ANSI Z39.48-1984. ∞

ISBN 0-89389-133-9

Dedicated to His Holiness Jagadguru
Sri Shivarathri Deshikendra Mahaswamigalu

Contents

INTRODUCTION:

Why Are Families Important?

I was raised and educated in the cave monasteries of the Himalayas and my "family" was my Master, a great sage who raised me from the age of three, after my parents had died. My master was both mother and father to me, and in my entire life, I have not met anyone since who has exhibited such complete love and dedication—he did everything possible for my welfare, and he never took anything for himself.

At times I have felt some sadness, because there was nothing I could give him to fully express my appreciation. He would never even accept a flower from me as a gesture of love. To me, he was the living example of unconditional love and selflessness. Throughout my training with him, he expressed his love in many diverse ways, which changed as I grew. Whatever good I have achieved in life actually belongs to him. He was the perfect parent, able to give total acceptance, and yet also to be honest and stern with me when I needed correction.

At times I was a nuisance; as a young child, I was sometimes naughty when I wanted his attention, and I distracted him from the depths of his meditation, but he accepted the responsibility of training me with love. This loving relationship provided the foundation of my life, and it is how I understand the great power that parents have to guide and help their children on the path of life.

In the years since I left the Himalayas, the place where my education began, I have traveled in the world, teaching and conducting research, and in the process, learning by observing the lives of thousands of people, both those who reside in families and those who have withdrawn from the conventional worldly life. I met hundreds of great souls in my travels, particularly in those remote mountain areas where there still dwell genuine sages, who continue to guide and lead mankind by their presence.

I have also met those who inhabit monasteries throughout the world, and have many times been disappointed, for some of those who take up this life do so from fear of accepting responsibility. Other times I have observed hypocrisy and arrogance in these supposedly holy people, as well as egotism about their status, which creates barriers between themselves and others. I did not observe the capacity to love and serve humanity. I visited monasteries all over the world, but I eventually came to the regretful conclusion that some of the greatest hypocrites of all time lived in those monasteries. I was so disappointed and disillusioned that I thought, "What good is this life, if people are living so falsely? Why should people meditate or pray twelve hours a day if they are avoiding their responsibilities and developing enormous egos, rather than becoming more loving and selfless?"

And in the last several decades, all over the world, I have also observed many families as I traveled and taught. Couples have spoken to me of their marriages and their frustrations and successes. I have studied many kinds of families—happy and unhappy, poor and rich, young families, couples without children, and divorced parents raising children alone. I have met people whose lives were miserably poor but who gave their children everything they could—all the love and attention they could provide. And I have met couples who came to see me together, smiling and praising their partner with sweet words, while they were thinking of meeting with another man or woman. Sometimes these experiences made me very sad for the family.

I also talked with many sincere people who sought to follow a spiritual path while creating loving family lives in the world. Sometimes I have found in these married people a greater level of spiritual awareness and sincerity than in those who live monastic lives. There are many sincere and dedicated people in the modern world, East and West, who are trying to follow the path of a practical spirituality. They meditate and also fulfill their responsibilities to their partners, children, and the society in which they live through their selfless, active lives. Whenever I wanted to know whether a couple I met was genuinely happy and content, I would tell them, "You seem to be very happy," and then the reaction on their faces would tell me whether they were truly loving with each other, or whether their polite behavior was only superficial.

I have also seen many changes in the past twenty years, both in the East and in the West. There is increasing violence everywhere in the world, a crumbling of the foundations of the society, which creates many problems—rising rates of divorce and family conflict, problems with alcohol and drugs, and the inability to raise healthy, balanced children. There is also a pattern of greater stress, which challenges the physical and emotional health of even those who do not exhibit the most disastrous social problems. We look at our world and wonder how we will create peace and freedom. We want to successfully fulfill our responsibility to educate and train the children, those tender buds, who are given to us to nurture and raise.

In answering these questions it is clear that family life is important, because the foundation for life is established in childhood, especially in the first seven years. This sets a pattern for the duration of our lives. A great man once said, "Give me only the first seven years of life; the rest you can take." He meant that these first years are of the greatest importance in determining the course of life.

If childhood is healthy, then we have established a good foundation as human beings, and we are able to care for ourselves, contribute to society, and share our love with others. This means that we can also take the next step in life, the step of being able to explore the spiritual dimension of ourselves. However, if these first years of childhood are unhealthy, then they create problems and conflicts that we must overcome later in our lives, and which may even interfere with our ability to attain our goal. It is possible to resolve these problems and conflicts, although to do so may consume much of our adult lives. But life is like a school, and we cannot go on to the next level until we have completed the basic lessons. Families are the central training grounds for the entire life, the first step in a child's spiritual development. Parents are their children's first gurus, and if they complete their duties wisely, then the child moves on to other levels of learning.

Many of those who are sincerely pursuing the path of spirituality are parents. This role is of great importance in life, not only for the future welfare of the child, but also because taking on the responsibilities of parenthood and marriage can have such significant effects on the parents.

Some people enter into the responsibilities of marriage and parenthood with great wisdom, recognizing the importance of the duties and challenges they are accepting as part of their growth. Others have little insight or understanding of the real meaning of this task. They think that marriage and parenthood exist as institutions to make them happy and to satisfy their emotional desires. They think that all their relationships exist only for the pleasure they can provide. The most profound pleasures of parenthood are experienced when parents love their children without expectation of reward. Actually, family life is the most practical, psychologically satisfying way of living that human beings have yet devised. And relationships can provide many joys, especially the joy of watching children grow.

I love to see the children as I travel; they are so pure and their faces are so open and honest. Children are a delight to me. They are so pure that if you love and accept them, they know it and respond, and if you don't love them, they also know it. If you want to see the image of the living God, you can see it in the faces of children.

Children are sensitive to things that many other people cannot perceive, especially when they are very young, because they have not yet learned to lie and conceal the truth. But by the time they are older, they have developed this sense of false self, especially in families where they did not feel loved or safe.

Throughout my life, I have observed many great souls who have all loved children. Gandhi used to love to play with children; they would run to him and make noises in his face and play games, and adults would try to keep the children from bothering him, but he would reply, "Leave us alone; I am playing with my friends." For a person who has the capacity to love and see the divine within, the greatest joy in the world is a child. Children reflect their inner beauty so freely; they are the most entertaining companions. Sometimes modern parents seem to be unable to appreciate this beauty, perhaps because adults are so stressed and rushed in the modern world that they have no time to enjoy the best part of their lives.

This process is important for parents, because in parenting and being a loving partner there is a tremendous opportunity to make spiritual progress. The process of living in a family can teach us to become more loving, open, accepting, and selfless. When we love we can see the Self of all in the faces of those we love. We can work to remove the limitations of our own petty egotism by challenging ourselves to accept and serve others without selfishness. Those parents who knowingly accept this challenge and meet it wisely can achieve levels of personal maturity, wisdom, serenity and love as a result of their learning in the family. The path of spirituality develops as you learn to love and continually expand that capacity to love, from your spouse and family to your community, to your nation and eventually the entire world.

I often say that there are two competing processes in life, which determine the entire course of a person's spiritual growth and evolution. One process is the tendency toward contraction, in which a person becomes increasingly selfish, bitter, egotistical, and separate from others in life. No matter how much such people pray or meditate, they can never make real spiritual progress if they continue to create walls between themselves and others. They can never recognize the essence in themselves or others. Contraction means hatred and fear; it reflects the absence of love and peace.

The second process is vital, for it is the process of expansion, the opening and development of love and the ability to recognize the essence in all. Only through expansion can a person ever really achieve happiness. Family life exists to help bring about expansion—to teach you to love. When you are alone in life you love only yourself. Then you meet and love your partner, and eventually you learn to love your children. Throughout life this love expands, extending in wider and wider circles. Family life is a preparation to accept and love the whole of humanity.

Those who undertake their relationships from this perspective can fulfill their duties happily, leaving no pieces of their work undone. We can say that they fulfill their karmas in a beneficial way. *Karma* is a word that is much used but still misunderstood in the West. It simply refers to the Law of Cause and Effect: as you sow, so shall you reap. If we successfully and lovingly carry out our responsibilities in the world, we complete a stage of life.

Then, when children are grown and leave the home to create new families, no conflicts, resentments or lingering regrets remain. All the family members move on to their next stage with a sense of gratitude and respect for those who contributed to their learning.

Sometimes parents forget that their children are also meant to be their spiritual teachers, as much as any person who teaches meditation. Children are spiritual teachers because they help you to see and become aware of your personality and inner tendencies. If you are a sincere person who loves your children, you will want to eliminate any negative, hurtful tendencies in your personality that interfere with your ability to guide your children. Since these negative, hurtful tendencies are also the chief obstacles to your own progress spiritually, your children illustrate for you the domain of your spiritual work.

The path of loving relationships is the path of the heart, rather than the path of the mind or intellect. The intellect can be very helpful in certain kinds of progress in the external world, but there is one thing that the mind can never do: it can never create peace, since that is not its nature. If the mind and ego become too powerful, they can even interfere with a seeker's spiritual path, sometimes with disastrous results. In my travels I have met some great intellectuals whose family lives were miserable—full of bitterness and resentment. I have also found this tendency in some who profess to be capable of deep states of meditation. But if you observe their family lives, you see evidence of another sort. The test of genuine spiritual progress is simple: the capacity to love and serve all, and to hate or exclude none. If you cannot do this in your own family, then what kind of progress have you attained?

Love has enormous power, especially the love of a parent for his or her child. One time, many years ago, I was in a place called Rajgiri in India. During those days I would walk barefooted in the wilderness. As I walked along I met a mother and child who were going in the opposite direction. The mother was holding the child's hand as they walked. Suddenly a wild elephant charged forward and ran toward us all. Without an instant's hesitation, the mother gently pushed the child behind her and stood alone facing the elephant. She said firmly, "Stop there!" and the elephant stopped! The depth with which a mother can love her child is a special thing; a mother loves her child so much that she doesn't fear any danger to herself. That's the greatest solace in human life—this real symbol of love.

Other times, people who have expanded their personalities with love have tremendous power to help even those who are not part of their family. Perhaps you have seen examples of this: a home is in flames and a mother and father are weeping outside on the sidewalk. Their child is inside the burning home and they cannot rescue her, even though they love the child. Suddenly a stranger comes along and is overwhelmed with a feeling of empathy for the child who is left all alone in the burning home. He runs into the fire and brings the child outside, even though he is in danger of being burned by the flames. For a while he does not fear any pain because of his tremendous emotion for that child. His heart goes out to that child and he willingly risks his own life. Such a person has expanded his love to others, and has achieved something great.

In this simple book I have tried to share candidly and

straightforwardly my perspective on marriage and parent-hood, the result of my training in the tradition of medita-tion, as well as my experiences in the modern world. My goal is to help those who are seeking ways to make their families more loving. If those who are on the spiritual path understand the meaning of family life, it will help them to skillfully and joyfully complete this phase of their life. In other books I have taught some of the specific practices of meditation and holistic health, which are referred to in this volume. May these practical guidelines and ideas help all readers make their family lives more harmonious and joyful.

CHAPTER 1

Creating a Loving Commitment

Before I learned about marriage, parenthood or the development of an average social being who lives in the world, I lived in the Himalayan mountains for many years. At the age of three, I had been adopted by a great swami and yogi who became my teacher, and I lived with him in the mountains during my entire childhood. I did not know anything about the external world, but I was well trained in meditation. After I finished my schooling, I was invited to speak on the topic of married life at one of the major universities of India. My lecture was based on what I had learned from books and my teachers. A woman in that class challenged me, "Are you married?" When I told her that I was not, she got up to leave the class, saying, "Well, if you have never experienced married life, then how can you teach other people about it?" She had a point, and I took that point to heart.

The more I traveled in the world, the more curious I

became about marriage and family life, and I started to study married life by observing closely how couples live and speak together. Sometimes I have been very disappointed, for all over the world I have found that many people have not yet learned to live skillfully with others. More than anything else, it is a problem of people not adjusting to each other and to the realities of family life. We do not know how to adjust ourselves to each other chiefly because we usually do not have any clear goal in life. If we shared a clear goal in life, we could understand how to adapt to each other and create harmonious families.

Human beings are social beings; we cannot possibly live entirely without contact with others. Even those who have adopted a monastic life need social relationships. From what I have observed, to be alive as a human being means having relationships; life and relationships are synonymous. The first relationship a person has is with his or her mother. A child loves his mother in a limited, immature way, because she pays constant attention to him and does things for him constantly. Beyond this love for the mother, the nature of a child's "love" is limited to self love.

By their natures, young children are initially selfish, and through the process of living with other family members and learning to understand them, children gradually evolve beyond their self-preoccupation, developing the capacity for deeper love. Later, children realize that they could not survive without the help of many others. A child learns that without relationships, life would remain empty. First, the child's capacity to love expands towards its mother and then gradually toward others. The nature of love is to continually expand throughout life.

Genuine love means service done for others. Our deeds are the real expressions of our love. When we do something for others without any thought of return or reward, then we have evolved beyond the limitations of our individuality. Otherwise, we are trapped in our individuality forever; we think about ourselves, talk about ourselves, and want to fulfill our own desires. In our daily lives, we are not yet fully aware of other human beings. But genuine love is the opposite of selfishness.

If you really want to see clearly the person you love, it is helpful to observe how much that person does for you. Then you can ask, "But how much am I doing selflessly for the one I claim to love?" This issue is a yardstick by which you can measure yourself. When people study and observe themselves from this perspective, then they can discover how much they are really capable of loving others.

Some people think that many men and women turn to married life only for the sake of security, motivated by selfishness and the fear of being alone. Actually, the institution of marriage exists for a much higher purpose; it is not simply a biological or emotional convenience. The great sages teach that marriage is more sacred than a mere contract or arrangement in which two people decide to get together and live with each other. Marriage has a goal, and both partners should have a common purpose, regardless of the country from which they come or their cultural, religious, philosophical or historical backgrounds. Everyone seeks happiness in life, but the problem is, how do we achieve a state of genuine happiness in the world, when everything around us is changing constantly? Whatever makes us happy will not last forever. This external world of people and objects is transient and impermanent. So how does a human being achieve a state of enduring happiness?

Most people wait for others to make them happy, and they think that at some specific point they will achieve happiness—when they are married or a child is born or they purchase a home. But none of these joyful events creates lasting happiness. Thus, the mind itself creates suffering, because it harbors expectations that are unrealistic—

the only real happiness lies within.

We expect marriage or family life to make us happy, but this institution is not the goal itself, it is only a means to a deeper happiness. If two people share this understanding, then they can enjoy their married life with a sense of contentment, rather than expectation.

The highest aim of life is to possess the deeper happiness that is eternal, undisturbed, and unchanging. To achieve such happiness, human beings need to understand not only themselves but others as well.

In ancient times men and women did many experiments and finally decided to live together with a certain understanding in the arrangement that we call marriage. In Persian the word for marriage is *cushy*, which also means "happiness." In Sanskrit the word for marriage is *vivaha*, which signifies that two people have decided to tread their paths together and attain the highest state of happiness in this lifetime.

But I have observed that all too often, marriage does not lead to such happiness. Rarely have I seen a genuinely happy couple. Couples often come to see me smiling and I feel very happy when they affirm their love for one another. The first question I ask them is whether they love each other, and they usually insist that they do, but often after some time passes, I discover that their claims are false. I have tried to understand the root cause of this superficial level of commitment and insincere life, and I have found that the cause lies in their individual selfishness.

When people decide to marry, they need to recognize that up to that point, they have lived alone, which is easy, because a single person can think only of himself or herself. Now, they must learn to live with each other. People who wish to marry should ask themselves, "Do I have the capacity to live intimately with this person? Can I adjust to him or her? Do I have the essential qualities that are

CREATING A LOVING COMMITMENT 15

needed to live with others—truthfulness, sincerity, faithfulness, tolerance, patience, acceptance, and self-sacrifice? Do I have the qualities that I will need to live peacefully with another person? If not, I must develop them, or I will not succeed in my marriage."

Modern society is still engaged in a process of social and interpersonal experimentation, exploration, and inquiry. It is attempting to discover the goal of human life. Each individual also makes his or her own experiments, not with society as a whole, but with another person. A person first learns to live with those closest to him or her. If a man does not yet know how to live with his wife pleasantly and lovingly, he is mistaken if he thinks that he can become a great man. If a person cannot live peacefully with one other person, how can he or she live harmoniously with all of humanity?

Sometimes, after several years of marriage, a couple decides that they have committed a mistake and now want to divorce each other. Everyone encounters difficulties and challenges in marital life, but that does not mean that the answer is ending the marriage. In every marriage there are misunderstandings that can be rectified if you decide to do so. Difficulties can be resolved when two people understand and learn to accept each other.

When you live strictly as an individual, you understand only yourself. Your whole mind, body, actions, and speech are geared to an awareness of your own ego and its needs and desires. But the goal of marriage is to learn to expand your understanding and sensitivity to your partner.

There is a level of our being that is more profound and evolved than our bodies. When we understand and become aware of our deeper existence, that awareness leads to a state of union and true marriage between two people, which is not based on externals.

In the modern world, living with one person for a long time is sometimes considered to be a kind of torment or hardship. Change is considered to be interesting, exciting, and beneficial. People get bored or frustrated with each other. When this happens, they think, "Why should I live with this person?"

It has become easier and more attractive to end a marriage than to work sincerely to improve the relationship. This societal tendency of modern men and women to casually end marriages because they do not wish to give up their selfishness has caused a great deal of damage, particularly to children. It is a very tragic thing for children that people will now readily end a marriage, rather than making a sincere effort to improve the relationship. Of course, if one partner is causing harm, sometimes the other must leave, but this should never be a casual choice or a first attempt. Our society should help people learn to improve or repair a damaged marriage.

When people who have seen this phenomenon try to apply this idea in India or other traditional cultures, society prevents them. If a husband thinks of divorcing his wife, then his wife, his relatives, and the entire community become upset with him. There is no escape for such a person in other parts of the world! In that situation individuals definitely suffer, but society as a whole seems to suffer less, because the family unit remains intact. In the East most people still believe that the institution of marriage should be strengthened and preserved so that children and the society do not suffer and so that marriage can provide an opportunity to attain the purpose of life. In both the Jewish and Hindu cultures, the role of women has kept the respective communities alive and strong for a long time. In these traditions the family unit is primary. This does not mean that people don't quarrel; they suffer and fight just as much as other people and do the same things that might lead to divorce in a modern marriage.

Of course, it can also cause problems if couples remain married due to social pressure without seeking to establish a genuine understanding. The ideal is for both partners to commit themselves to improving the relationship.

I have never seen a child grow up without some disturbance or confusion if the parents become divorced. A divorce creates guilt, fear, and great sadness for children. Children of a tender age do not understand what has happened. When I ask the children how they feel about it, sometimes they say, "It's fine with me," and when I ask why, they reply, "I live with my Mom and get toys and I also get toys from my Dad. When they both lived together, they did not give me as many things. But I don't understand why they can't live together."

There always seems to be some conflict in the children's minds. Of course, there are circumstances in which divorce is unavoidable, but adults should not casually undertake a divorce for their own selfish purposes without considering their children's welfare. When adults realize that life does not exist only to satisfy their physical and emotional needs, perhaps they will learn to tolerate and adjust to each other, and divorce will not be so prevalent. If adults enter marriage with a deep and mature commitment, the best answer is for them to correct and improve the relationship.

The highest guiding principle in marriage should be the principle of selfless service to one's partner. Selfless action alone is the real expression of love. The opposite of selfless love is having expectations and making demands. The greatest mistake that we make in relationships is that we have so many expectations of each other.

Young people, in particular, often expect too much from marriage: they think that once they are married they will achieve fulfillment in life. Young girls think that they will marry the man of their dreams and many men think that their wives will always seem like beautiful and loving princesses. But after a few months of marriage they realize with a shock that the person they have married cannot live up to their fantasies. They become disappointed after a short time, regret their decision, and think that they have made a mistake. The real mistake is in expecting too much from marriage in the first place, rather than recognizing that the purpose of marriage is to learn to live selflessly.

Many couples come to me for counseling saying, "What can we do? There is no way out. We have made a mistake." They don't realize that marriage has limitations; it can only give people so much, but they expect everything from it. Yet if people approached marriage realistically, there are many things that they could explore and discover in the process, and marriage could be just a beginning point in that growth.

I don't think that anyone should be in a hurry to marry. Marriage is not a biological necessity. The sexual drive is a biological reality and necessity, but marriage is not. These are two different issues; sex is an act and marriage is an understanding. Ideally, these two should go hand-in-hand, but if people marry for the sake of having a sexual partner, they don't really understand the purpose of life. The necessity for marriage arises when a person wants to learn more about how to relate to others and how to experience joy in doing things for others. It is possible to learn those lessons when a close relationship is created.

If two people decide to live together, it is important for them to first have an overall goal and aim in life. It is easy to create goals; we all talk about our goals. Many young people who get married think about material goals: "We will buy a house, a car, and we'll have good jobs." But what happens after that? Perhaps you buy a nice car and someone of the opposite sex is attracted to you and wants a ride in your car. Perhaps you suddenly become infatuated with that person and are swayed by that temptation. Where does this fit with your overall aim in life? Apart from the usual material goals, you need to have a deeper, overriding purpose in life to help you deal with such dilemmas. A couple should ask, "Why are we getting married? Can we help each other toward our ultimate goal?"

When modern marriage does not create a common life with a shared purpose, something called an "open marriage" may be substituted. I have met many couples who said, "We have a free or open marriage." For the first few years that I lived in the West, I didn't really understand this phrase, so one day I asked, "What do you mean by a free marriage?"

The woman said, "It means I can do what I want, and he can do what he wants."

I still didn't understand.

People explained, "Perhaps, Swami, you cannot understand this because you are from India."

I replied, "I would really like to understand this; please keep explaining."

Finally the woman said, "I can sleep with anybody, and he can also sleep with anybody; we are not committed to each other—that's what a free marriage means!"

At a very young age, perhaps people can afford to live like that. There is no need to marry if that is all a couple wants, since the institution of marriage is not meant merely to satisfy sexuality, but to fulfill a larger aim. That is why the great scriptures say that marriage is an institution arranged in heaven and performed on earth. It is not merely a contract or an understanding; a couple who are married are like the two wheels of a chariot, which roll together toward a shared goal.

Before they are married, it is important for a couple to discuss their goals and try to understand each other's ways. Each person should be willing to become aware of and sensitive to someone apart from himself or herself. We carry our own individual awareness with us constantly, but this is not a complete awareness. Even animals know that they exist, but we would not really call that awareness. To be aware merely that "I exist" is not a deep level of awareness; that is simply an instinct, which all human beings, animals, insects, and other creatures have.

Real awareness is gained when one person becomes aware of something apart from himself or herself, in the same way and to the same depth and sensitivity that one is aware of one's own needs and feelings. Then a person begins to respect the other's existence as much as one's own. This leads a person to realize that all human beings deserve the same rights, and to wonder, "Why should I deprive others of their rights?" This realization is the first step toward developing a genuine sensitivity and deeper human consciousness.

Often we try to change others—even our friends or those we claim to love. This is one of the greatest defects or failings in our companionships in the world. In many marriages the woman wants to change her husband and the husband wants to change his wife. We marry our mates for their uniqueness and then we want them to be like us. If the husband drinks alcohol and goes to parties, he wants his wife to drink and socialize as he does. If she cannot do that, he thinks that she is inferior or has failed somehow. Such an attitude is very destructive; a successful marriage can only be founded on an acceptance of one's partner.

Psychologists often place the blame for our current problems on our childhoods. Sometimes, this is because they cannot find any solutions for them in the present. If you don't know how to relate well to your wife, you go to a psychologist, who may say, "These problems come from your childhood," but this is not necessarily the only way to look at it. The seeds of certain problems are sown in childhood, but many other problems stem from our present outlook and attitudes. Some sexual problems should not be thought of as childhood problems at all, but should be understood in terms of the present circumstance. Once you adopt this perspective, many problems can be corrected. Some problems are based on unbalanced emotionality; if the partners don't understand what emotional self-control and balance are, there will be differences between them that create incompatibility. When there is understanding, love, and patience, people can help one another, adjust to each other, and correct their problems and misunderstandings.

I know a man whose wife divorced him because he was impotent. On the physical level, there was nothing wrong with him, but there were many problems in the relationship. A person may become impotent or averse to intimacy in one circumstance but not in others. An interest in sexual intimacy depends on the person's emotions and attractions or aversions. If a man has lost interest in his wife and has become cold, he may become impotent. The same principle applies to a woman if she does not feel emotionally open to being sexual. Many cases of impotence or sexual difficulty are due to internal emotional distress or conflict in the relationship, rather than physical problems.

When we have an aim or purpose in life, we can bring our emotional life under control. But no one besides ourselves can help us become aware of our purpose in life; we must discover it directly. Priests or ministers can suggest that we become aware of God, and if a person believes there is some higher force that will help them, these words may provide solace when a person feels helpless. But words of solace are not the same as having a direct experience. To provide real solace and comfort, people need to experience undisturbed peace and happiness from within.

We all want to experience a state of freedom from pain and miseries. Unfortunately, instead of relying upon our inner resources, we often rely upon sources outside ourselves and stop making our own sincere personal efforts. We forget that "God helps those who help themselves." As a result, we fail to realize our potential and do not make progress. When we become aware of our innate, divine nature, we can attain a state of freedom from all fears, pains, and miseries. We can realize that happiness within ourselves and eventually learn to share that happiness with others.

When we study the lives of great men and women, we notice that one thing they have in common is the apparent experience of suffering. What these great ones experience would be suffering for most people, but to them, it is a joy. To us, it seems that Jesus suffered a great deal in his brief life, but actually he chose his life, and for him it was not a life of suffering, but one of purpose. We common people might call it suffering because our mind's capacity to understand is limited by our selfishness. To us, the great people of the world seem to have suffered, because our narrow vision and understanding can only perceive it as such.

If a person is really intent on expanding his or her mind, then it is necessary to let go of the narrow boundaries and mental constraints that have been developed. For example, many people have acquired the constraint of thinking that they can only be happy within certain conditions or limitations. But happiness cannot be achieved by setting conditions or building boundaries; happiness means expansion and expansion means love. Love includes a willingness to serve. A person who truly loves, serves others selflessly.

In loving, we expand ourselves and become aware of the reality that just as we exist, others also exist. Then as we grow and become more sensitive, we ask ourselves why we are cruel, and how we can become more loving. We need and want love from others; can we learn to love them as well? When people begin to contemplate how they can become more loving, then their homes will become centers of love, places that radiate love to others. It can never work to have only material goals in a marriage, such as having a winter home in Miami, or having two cars or a good bank balance. Thinking in that manner can never help to keep a marriage together over the many years and challenges of life.

If you are curious about the quality of someone's family life, you can do an experiment—ask that person what his or her attitude is as they come home from work at the end of a day. When someone smiles naturally in response to this question, then I know that this person's home life is happy. There is at least one place where they enjoy peace and harmony. If a husband is greeted lovingly and comforted when he returns home, he experiences happiness and pleasure at being home. Children who have loving homes are happy to return to their parents after school.

Those who have such loving homes always look forward to returning home. When they go to their offices, they think pleasantly about returning to their spouses and children. But those whose homes are disturbed and unpleasant think of going to bars or other places of escape. Such a person thinks, "At five o'clock, I will go to a bar for a drink. What a wretched life I have at home. I wish I could meet someone else." Thus, two people of a similar dissatisfied frame of mind will often meet. Both are disturbed, and as they share their disturbance, they become even unhappier. If a person is miserable, what he or she shares with another miserable person is never happiness.

Once, many years ago, I was visiting East Africa and was invited to stay in the guest house of an Indian businessman who was very successful and controlled cashew commodities around the world. I said to the couple, "God bless you; you both seem to be happy," but as I said this, I noticed that his wife saddened. That was actually my way of finding out whether or not they were truly happy. By simply making the statement, I learned from the expression on their faces whether or not it was true.

At dinner that evening, the table was full of tasty dishes, but I couldn't relish the food, for I didn't sense any aliveness or joy in the house, and yet the wife was a beautiful woman with gracious manners. In her presence, her husband said to me, "She is called Grihalakshmi, meaning the 'Goddess of the Home.' "

Later I said to her privately, "Your husband respects and appreciates you very much."

But she laughed bitterly and said with disgust, "You have come here as a swami, so it is your duty to tell my husband not to be a hypocrite in what he says, but to treat his wife honestly and sincerely. Ask him where and with whom he spends his time! Please do that for me."

When I spoke to him, the husband said, "My wife is beautiful and my house has all the latest conveniences, but I am not happy here. Do you know what she does to me? She nags me so much that I don't ever want to come home."

When a woman becomes lonely and feels neglected, she may project her unhappy feelings onto a man, making accusing and critical statements, but she often does not mean everything she says. The husband arrives home tired from the day's work, and when he hears these negative things he says to himself, "I'll just come home late and go to sleep, then get up early in the morning and leave for work." In this home, there were two people living together pretending to be a happily married couple, but they were not truly married. Nagging and hypocrisy don't create a loving life with anyone.

Another time many years ago I encountered a situation in rural India that was the opposite of what I have just described, but it was an equally poor relationship. In traditional Indian culture, there is a custom of touching the feet of someone we respect and revere, such as our parents. There was a wife who used to touch her husband's feet ten times a day, and that man became very inflated with pride, because he actually had a weak, inadequate personality. Outside his home, nobody respected him at all, so he sought to receive such gestures of respect from his wife.

I asked him, "Are you really comfortable when your wife bows before you and touches your feet? Do you need her to do that for you?"

He replied, "Of course, a woman should always show respect for her husband!"

I replied, "But I don't think you, yourself, are a truly happy or contented person, or you would not behave in this way."

Then he told me, "My wife is not my equal, because she is a simple, uneducated person. She's illiterate, and she doesn't know anything; she isn't very intelligent."

When I heard this I was very disappointed and became angry with his egotism. I replied, "You fool, your ego and arrogance are the problem. Your wife has emotions and a heart just like yours. You should have respect for her as a person!"

To have a happy marriage, it isn't necessary for both people to be intellectuals. Marital happiness has nothing to do with the mind. Actually, even if both partners were brilliant, they might simply fight and argue exactly the way people do in the legislatures. Everyone knows what happens in legislative debates: two intellectuals discuss a situation for several years, and they never succeed in passing a bill or reaching a conclusion. If two intellectuals in a marriage go on debating and arguing about how they want to build a house, the house will never be completed, and it will never become a home.

Marriage does not require that type of companionship. The quality of the relationship between a husband and wife depends on their love and commitment, not on the degrees they have received from the university. What a woman can give to a man, a man can never attain any other way, and what a man can give to a woman, she cannot attain elsewhere. If both partners understand the potential of that relationship, then a man and woman can live together skillfully and happily, for all the years of their marriage.

When people consider marriage they should ask themselves as individuals, "Can I live with this person happily? Can I make him or her happy?" Unfortunately, we often ask, "Can he or she make me happy?" which is the wrong way to think. The question itself is selfish. If you ask, "Do you love me?" it means, "I am not able to love you; I'm a very selfish person, but I expect love from you."

Married life is a commitment that must be made with one's full heart and mind. This commitment must be made from the depth of one's being, rather than taken lightly. If you undertake marriage lightly or without sincerity, it will never succeed. And when marriages fail to become centers of love, the whole society becomes disturbed. If marriages fail to create love, society disintegrates and returns to a violent and primitive level. Then there is no harmony or peace. When individual marriages become centers of love, they produce love that radiates to others. The members of such families have the capacity to love and serve others, and thereby help to transform the entire society.

CHAPTER 2

Developing Spiritual Intimacy

From the beginning of history there have been two major paths that people have taken in life in order to seek the goal of a deeper happiness and peace. A few sincere souls have decided to genuinely renounce the world's attractions in order to attain the highest wisdom. The path of renunciation actually means not keeping or possessing anything for oneself. Instead, these wise ones serve others, knowing that by doing so they are utilizing their time and energy in the best way. Living their lives in service to others is the characteristic by which you will recognize them.

Most people, however, still experience strong and compelling attractions to many things. They want to fulfill the desires for marriage, parenthood, and the conventional life. Thus, there is a second path, which is traveled by most people in the world, called the path of action. Throughout history, there has been confusion about which of these paths is superior.

27

A story is told to help clarify this confusion. Once, an arrogant swami, who had meditated in the mountains for many years, boasted about his spiritual advancement, thinking that he was superior to householders. He came down from the mountains to exhibit the powers he had gained in his studies. He had such a powerful gaze that if he looked at a bird flying overhead, its wings would catch fire and burn, and the bird would fall to the ground. He was very egotistical about his supposed spiritual power.

Eventually in his travels, he came to the home of a couple and he said rudely to the woman, "I want food, and I have no time to waste. It is your duty to feed me because I devote all my time to the Lord."

The woman, who was serving her husband's dinner at the time, said to him quietly but firmly, "Right now, I am doing my duty toward my husband lovingly, but don't ever make the mistake of thinking that I am as powerless as that bird you killed! I have far more power than you; if you think that you can hurt me, you are mistaken!"

The swami was stunned to realize that she had acquired the power to know many things about him while she was still living in the world, doing her duties as a wife. He fell at her feet and said, "Mother, clearly I have yet to understand the path of the world. Now I see that it, too, is a great path."

But the swami was not unusual; many people do not realize the power of family life. This is a path of living in the world, loving others, and also seeking and attaining the highest wisdom. Some people who want to follow the spiritual path are not content with their lives in the world. They do not appreciate how the path of marriage and parenthood helps them to fulfill life's ultimate purpose.

The path of a human being is not meant to be that of a loner who travels through life by himself or herself. If we want to express the meaning of life in a single sentence, it is that life means having relationships. Without relationships, life has no significance at all. The closest relationship in the world is that between a wife and husband, and the next most intimate relationship is that between parents and children.

Sometimes people wonder why the institution of the family was established. Marriage and family relationships do not exist merely because of the biological necessities of sex or childbirth. There is something deeper, which is responsible for the establishment of family life and which differentiates humans from animals. The most basic urges and drives that influence human life are also found throughout the animal kingdom, but there is an important difference between human beings and animals: the life and behavior of animals are primarily controlled by the forces of nature and instinct, but the life of a human being is not controlled this way. Instead, human beings are controlled mostly by mind, emotions, and by relationships. A human being thinks, understands, communicates, and participates in life in ways that animals cannot share. All these special qualities originate in the institution of the family. The family exists in order to foster and cultivate these qualities in human beings.

When the human race learns to live as a family, then the world will finally attain the next stage of civilization and enlightenment. Families are meant to be centers of love, which radiate their love outward to other families. A family is meant to radiate only love, rather than hatred, jealousy, competition, or other negative emotions. When people understand this purpose and can share the experience, then they can create joy and peace throughout society. When peace reigns, there will no longer be hatred or disturbances between people, and the human mind will automatically be led upward, towards the highest center of consciousness.

The path of marriage and family life is not inferior to any other path, nor is marriage meant solely to express our biological or emotional needs. The purpose of marriage is to establish and teach the fundamental principles of society, so that all children can develop fully and the entire society can eventually attain a state of peace and happiness.

Homes are meant to be places where people create and preserve a state of serenity and peace. Homes exist to establish peace, so that every person can learn to radiate and share love. Our homes can satisfy many of our emotional needs and help us to learn to open our hearts. Homes are not places to create power struggles or ego battles. They are not places to demonstrate or show off our intellect. Some people use their mind and emotions in their homes destructively, arguing, judging others, or trying to establish control over others to satisfy their ego needs. That does not help us achieve the full potential of a home. When homes provide children with a chance to receive love and enjoy the experience of being loved, then children learn to share their love with others as well.

We all need to learn how to live in our homes and also how to live in the world outside the home. There are two different principles or concepts in life: You talk to your spouse and your business colleagues in different ways and on different levels. When you talk to your business associates, it is wise to be thoughtful and consider your doubts first, examining what people say carefully so that you protect yourself before you act. But at home, you should not maintain this attitude of skepticism, doubt or self-protectiveness. At home, you can express yourself openly and spontaneously; you can be completely yourself. In the family, you can develop a deep trust and intimacy that are not usually possible in the world outside. This is possible when we respect the special role of marriage in our lives.

Most of the established cultures of the world have a similar approach to marriage. They foster and encourage engagements between those who are preparing to marry.

Often, in this process, a ring is exchanged to symbolize the commitment. In the ancient scriptures, this custom is explained poetically and beautifully. When two people exchange rings at their engagement, it signifies that these two people are prepared to marry, and to make the deep commitment that marriage requires. They understand the symbol of the ring, in which the two separate ends of a band of metal come together to form a perfect, round ring. Traditionally, two people who become engaged to marry prepare themselves to remain within the circle of their love, which is symbolized by the ring. They are testing their commitment to the necessary adaptations of married life.

After the engagement is completed, the marriage ceremony takes place. Some people marry and go through this wedding ceremony because of its social meaning—weddings satisfy a superficial desire for fun, status, attention, and pleasure. Other people marry due to loneliness: they feel they are missing something in life and think that another person can end that loneliness. Such people betray each other by exclaiming, "Now I feel complete, because you are with me." People sometimes say this to satisfy each other's emotional needs, but because no one can fully satisfy all of another person's needs, both partners eventually become unhappy, and depression or anger may develop.

When two people want to marry, it is helpful if they decide to live together to truly share their lives, rather than merely to satisfy each other's material or biological desires. The first step of marriage is learning to share, and to share, couples need to appreciate the importance of the word *participation*.

For example, if your wife enjoys playing the piano, but you discourage her, telling her that you don't like to listen to her playing the piano, then a defect or weakness will be created in the marriage. You are not participating in her interests or letting her be herself. You are refusing to share what is important to her.

Then perhaps one day you will want to walk in the woods and will ask her to come with you, but she will say, "Why would you want to go there? I don't enjoy that." She will give you the same kind of treatment that you gave her. To succeed in marriage, you need to create an acceptance of each other's preferences as separate individuals.

Each person should learn to appreciate and admire the other's taste. If the husband likes to wear a particular style or color, his wife shouldn't try to criticize him or control his choices by telling him what to wear. If people try to appreciate the taste, aesthetic sense, and the hobbies of their partner, they can create real sharing. This is what it means to appreciate the other person and participate with him or her.

Often husbands do not take the time to share and communicate with their wives; they become excessively involved in their work while their wives wait for them at home. A woman whose husband does not participate in the marriage may begin to crave attention and emotional contact and feel frustrated in the marriage. When women become lonely or feel a lack of communication with their husbands, they may become emotional, eat or drink to excess, or seek fulfillment elsewhere. If a husband comes home feeling tired, and then withdraws from his wife and children by reading the newspaper, switching on the TV or even going to sleep, his wife may feel betrayed because he is treating her like a piece of furniture. Similarly, if a wife is not interested in her husband's feelings and the experiences that are important to him, he may feel she does not participate in his life.

Some husbands are away from home all day and do not share any meaningful time with their wives. They do not understand why there are problems in their relationships, but one part of the problem is that they fail to participate in communication or sharing. These days, both partners may work outside the home and have little time to talk or share their feelings.

Women often need a different kind of companionship and communication than men think they need. Some men want to demonstrate their virility through sexual contact, but they fail to understand that real communication requires something more. That physical experience alone doesn't satisfy a woman. When they talk about their marriages, women say that they want companionship, a sense of participation, and understanding. If a woman does not receive these in her marriage, she may react strongly. If she is weak or insecure, she may become depressed, and if she is stronger, she may lose her temper with her husband. Neither reaction helps the marriage; violent emotions can be as dangerous as suppressed emotions. A man should listen to his wife and try to understand her feelings, rather than making her suppress her feelings by asserting to her that her feelings are wrong.

Many modern marriages are unsuccessful because they lack a solid foundation; they are based on material success or the partner's physical charms and attractions. How many times a week can a couple have sex if there is no deeper communication? At first, this intimacy may be pleasant, but after some time, if there is no deeper sharing, people get bored and think that changing their partner is the solution to the problem. Married life can help people to regulate and balance their sexual urge by providing a healthy and satisfying sexual outlet, if they recognize that although sex is a biological necessity, marriage is meant to help couples attain a higher goal than mere biological needs.

Sometimes people ask me how husbands and wives can help each other in marriage. The most important way to help your spouse is by understanding and accepting that person. Allow them to be themselves and enjoy their personality.

When I studied marriages all over the world, I was

surprised to discover that many couples say they do not fully understand each other, even after they have lived together for forty years. This frequently happens because the husband thinks only of his own desires; he does not take the time to understand his wife's nature, preferences or viewpoint. But if he does not understand her, he cannot help her and she will not be satisfied or fulfilled in their relationship.

Understanding your spouse and accepting his or her feelings is a higher and more important step than simply satisfying the person's superficial desires. If your wife wants a new dress, you could say, "We have plenty of money, just go buy yourself a beautiful dress." But that isn't going to satisfy her; it isn't really what is important to her. Let her see that you are interested enough to participate in fulfilling her desires, and take a loving interest in the process.

Similarly, a wife can take an active role in appreciating her husband's interests and preferences. If he is interested in sports she may want to share some athletic activities with him or share time by appreciating his enthusiasms. Each partner should enjoy the other's interests and not be threatened by them.

There are several guidelines for establishing a healthy marriage. Understanding of these principles can help people to create stronger, more loving marriages. Those who are already married can begin to apply them and learn them in their present circumstances. The first principle is that a marriage is strongest and most satisfying if a couple forms a shared commitment and purpose. At some point, a couple can sit down together and renew the commitment they made to each other. "When we married, we did so with sincere intentions. Let us accomplish something important in life, creating a loving and sincere marriage by cooperating, participating fully, helping each other, and by admiring and appreciating each other."

The second principle is that both partners should accept each other as equals. Married life can become a companionship, without either partner feeling superior or inferior. A couple should marry and live together with a sense of equal status, rather than one partner treating the other as an inferior. I often tell people that if they do not respect their partner as an equal, there is something wrong with their own attitude. The basis of a marriage is love and acceptance, and that exists between equals.

In the first year of marriage there is often a continual struggle for power between the partners, as one tries to establish control over the other. Both tell their friends, "He is my husband; he should listen to me," or "She is my wife; she should do what I say." In this process, they consciously and unconsciously try to project their personalities onto each other. In doing this, they are acting from insecurity and seeking to expand their egos, because up to this point, they have lived their whole lives seeking only to fulfill their own ego needs. If this continues, it will eventually become difficult for them to adjust to each other. If the husband has a friend, his wife may condemn his friend; if she has friends, he may likewise criticize her friends. Each person wants to impose his or her personality on the other person, because both partners want to "own" or control someone; neither wants to share the other and accept the other's independence.

To avoid this power struggle, it helps to develop the mutual understanding from the very beginning: "We respect each other as equals. Let us try to appreciate and accept the other." Try to avoid relating to your partner by demanding, "I don't like this," or "I don't like that." If this is how you relate to each other, there are bound to be continual quarrels.

While it is easy for us to correct each other and analyze another person's faults, what gets in the way of our learning is our own egos. A man can learn from almost anyone but his wife; and a wife can often learn from anyone but her husband. For example, when I was in England many years ago, two great British actors came to ask for my blessing. They said, "Swami, please give us your blessing, we are getting married next week."

I said, "I bless everybody, but I feel uneasy about your request. You don't seem to be the marrying types. Perhaps you are making a mistake?"

They had both signed checks and wanted to give them to me; they wanted to pay me two thousand dollars for my "blessings." I said, "I can surely spend this money for the good of others, but I don't want to give you a blessing merely because you are paying money. Sit down and let's talk first; let me ask you, are you really getting married, or is this an arrangement? Is this a 'free' or 'open marriage'?" After living in the West for a while, I had learned about such classifications.

They replied, "We are both free to live anywhere, do what we want, and sleep with anybody."

I asked, "Then how is this marriage going to last? What is your commitment to each other? I don't need your money, and if you want to marry on such terms, I don't feel right about it. Please go to someone else who can bless you; my conscience does not allow me to do that."

"Why not?" they asked.

"Because you don't have any understanding of what you are doing. What you call grace—the grace of God—is with you, provided that you understand what marriage means, but there can never be grace in a home in which there is no understanding. You should have an understanding and sense of purpose that supports the aspects of life."

They got married seven days later, and it was televised on the news throughout Europe because they were very famous actors. But after a week, another news story was broadcast, revealing that they had separated and decided to divorce after a violent argument. The cause of the argument was nothing but a conflict between their egos; they fought about the issue of how to correctly handle the toothpaste tube, and eventually they got divorced. This entire conflict was about their attempts to control each other. This really happened; they were very bright, young, talented, and healthy people. They were sexually compatible, but sexual compatibility alone cannot lead to a successful marriage. If sex is the only thing that a couple has in common, eventually, a loss of interest or commitment will enter the marriage.

Throughout married life, the partners should increase their understanding and appreciation of each other. This understanding involves both people in talking and communicating, rather than arguing. When two people disagree, their disagreement may sometimes reach a height of emotion and they begin to argue heatedly. Their emotionality overcomes their reasoning, and where there is no reason, there is a fight. Partners sometimes become angry and dissatisfied with each other and yet continue to share the same bed.

It is dangerous to live together in the same house with disagreements, suppressions, and repressions, which influence both partners' unconscious minds. If disagreements or misunderstandings damage the relationship, rebuild your commitment and sense of understanding again and again in life. Partners need to learn to be tolerant, kind, and loving to each other; mutual understanding is based on acceptance, patience, and self-control.

Emotions are very powerful; when people become angry and lose their temper, they no longer know when they are wrong. Both behave stubbornly and impulsively because they think they are right. During such arguments it is helpful if one partner's role is to remain calm and not argue. If one person remains calm and tolerates the other's outburst for a few minutes, the other will usually say, "I'm sorry, I won't repeat that." Sometimes it is important to let your partner express his or her anger without overreacting. If each person can do this some of the time, there will be fewer ego-battles.

The goal is to develop understanding and tolerance. The most important trait needed in a marital relationship is tolerance. Decide to be aware of your feelings and remain tolerant, rather than arguing; no conclusion can ever be reached through arguments. You can learn to appreciate one another by talking to each other and trying to understand each other. Even if you do not agree with your spouse, try to understand the other's view.

It is not necessary to agree on every matter; all individuals have their own personal thoughts and emotions. Life would be dull if two people always agreed, but neither is it necessary to argue constantly. This is always a sign of egotism. Spouses can learn to talk things over; each should try to understand and accept the other's viewpoint. If, for example, you don't like to go out to dinner, inform your spouse, "I'm sorry, I don't want to go." Explain your feelings to your partner. If you have a genuine reason, you should not go. It is not necessary to quarrel. Home is the one place where people should be able to find and maintain peace.

When I meet a couple who smile sincerely, I always think, "God has graced them; they have created peace in their home." However, if that peaceful atmosphere is not already present in your home, you can still create it. Walls and objects do not radiate love and peace, but you can create and express those feelings and let them penetrate through thick walls—and keep doing it forever. In this way, a house can become a sweet home, a healthy center for living and mutual understanding.

Men have often called women the "weaker sex," or the "fair sex" but there is no such thing; women are an entirely *different* sex. The wife's and husband's roles are different, yet they can help each other by sharing their joys and experiences. The wife's role cannot be fully played by the husband, no matter what modern men and women think. The man should never allow the woman to lose her heart—her sensitivity and empathy—and the woman should never allow the man to lose his head. They can create a perfect understanding between them, so that they come together exactly like the two ends of the piece of gold metal that forms a ring.

Women have a hidden power that man can never fully understand. Biologically, women can often tolerate more pain than men, and women are much more resistant to stress and many other hardships. If you analyze medical data from all over the world, you will learn that only a small number of women have heart attacks. Biologically, women are "shock absorbers." They often endure suffering in ways men cannot. If a man has a small fever or a headache, he starts to cry for help, but women can withstand much more discomfort and pain.

A woman is a very powerful being. Unfortunately, women sometimes use their power to make men dependent, slowly and gradually. This is because woman is responsible for establishing and maintaining the institution of marriage. Throughout the ages, man has been irresponsible; it has always been the woman who has felt the necessity to establish a home when she foresaw the coming of a baby. A woman doesn't want to experience childbearing alone; she wants someone to help her bring up the child. Because of this, her strength is sometimes diverted toward creating dependency. She makes a man dependent by looking after him so much that he begins to see his mother's image in her. Then after some time, she may feel that he is no longer a real man, that he has become passive or weak. This is one of the greatest drawbacks in modern marriages.

These days there is often a discontinuity and lack of compatibility between a man's sexual feelings and a woman's sexual feelings. The failure of men and women to understand the differences in each other's sexual emotions and inclinations remains one of the primary causes of their disagreements. Modern people sometimes do not understand that woman is sensitive and receptive by nature; man is an active force. Women approach sex with love, consideration, tolerance, and a certain reserve. Men rapidly become sexually interested. They may rush to their wives and engage in sex abruptly, without adequate preparation, and then leave or go to sleep. Sometimes, a woman's feelings and interest only become active by the time the man has finished. Women talk about this problem with their friends and counselors; they want to feel affection and closeness before their sexual feelings become active.

Throughout the world, this lack of understanding has been one of the largest obstacles and problems in marriage. It often continues for the entire married life, because the man never really tries to understand the woman. A couple can produce many children, but this fact alone does not mean they have a real intimacy or sexual understanding. People do not need to be sexually competent to produce children. To be able to satisfy the biological urges, men have to understand that woman has a different nature—she wants love, sensitivity, and preparation. To achieve this, a man needs to be calm, mature, and self-controlled. In some marriages, a woman never expresses how disappointed she feels, but if by chance she eventually does so, the man may overreact. He may then become depressed or even impotent. Sometimes a woman hurts or wounds a man by making him feel inadequate. If a woman continually speaks that way to her man, she will destroy him emotionally.

How can men and women resolve this lack of understanding? Each should learn about the biological realities of life and how to deal with them appropriately and skillfully. This can only be accomplished through self-awareness and self-regulation. This self-regulation means that a couple comes to an understanding about how they will manage food, sleep, sex, and other activities. A couple usually decides how to manage their schedule and activities: "We will rise at a particular time; we will do our exercises; and we will eat dinner at a particular time." The experience of sex should be approached with a similar understanding: after an initial honeymoon, a couple should learn to regulate and prepare for their sexual life.

Sex should be done consciously and with a positive intent, rather than haphazardly or without preparation; the partners should agree on when they would like to reserve time to share and communicate in this way. There should be an agreeable understanding between spouses about how and when they want to be sexually active. After many years of studying and counseling couples from various countries on this subject, I have concluded that the best way is for the couple to decide upon a time for sexual companionship.

People are often confused about how the other person feels sexually, or what he or she wants. Sometimes they are too shy or insecure to express their desires. Sometimes a man does not understand that a woman may be exhausted from caring for small children all day. Sometimes the woman does not know what the man wants to do, and wonders whether he will want to have sexual relations. If a man is not considerate of his wife's feelings, or pressures her to have sex when she is tired or emotionally unprepared, many problems are created. This is not helpful, because fulfilling sexual interactions require mental preparation even more than physical readiness. If a woman is mentally and emotionally unprepared for sex, she freezes; if a man is preoccupied, nervous, or worried, he also has difficulty performing the sexual act. Both partners should be free from preoccupations or distractions. To prepare themselves and to create the proper mental and emotional environment, it is best to decide upon a time; then both partners can prepare and become emotionally and physically prepared at that time. Without such conscious preparation, a man often fails to satisfy the woman's needs.

Many traditional cultures provide guidelines about how to prepare emotionally and physiologically for sex. Timing is considered to be very important. Couples should allow enough time to digest their food before they engage in sex—an interval of about four hours between eating and sexual intimacy is helpful, especially if they have eaten a heavy meal. Or they should eat only food that is easy to digest. Many physical problems or difficulties occur when people eat food and then try to perform physically.

Secondly, the partners should also be well-rested. Such a powerful and important act should not be done abruptly, suddenly or in a hurry, because it is hard on the nervous system. In the modern world, some people think they need to drink alcohol for inspiration or preparation, but that is not a healthy pattern. Those who think that they need to drink alcohol to be sexually active often have conflicts about sexuality or emotional issues that they should resolve.

In my travels I have met many salesmen on airplanes and since I am a swami, they often talk candidly and reveal their secrets to me. Sometimes they talk about the subject of sexual relations, and I have observed how they think and how they live. Some men confess that they have sex wherever they go, but that they actually only enjoy it with their wives. They feel this way because the sexual act is not a mere physical or emotional animal act; when done with the proper understanding, it can become a spiritual flame of love.

Why shouldn't a man or woman indulge in sex with many partners? The reason this is so important is that sex is not merely a bodily function; sexual feeling actually originates in the mind, and sexuality affects the mind first and foremost. Many competing images and impressions are created in the mind if sex is performed randomly and without discrimination or self-control. The more partners a person has had, the more a person becomes mentally restless and desirous of even more different experiences. But none of these experiences can ever be fully satisfying. Eventually a time comes when that person becomes so distracted that he or she cannot enjoy the sexual act or remain faithful to one person. Such a disturbed condition can create a serious problem because the person becomes unable to live fully and deeply with a partner. It is better to discipline and limit yourself to one person, and learn to adjust your feelings, thoughts, and behavior so that the biological need may be satisfied and does not interfere with your life. Sexual fulfillment is a good thing, but sexuality alone is not the essence or purpose of life; there is something more important than sex.

What does sexual interaction provide? The physical experience gives people pleasure, but this pleasure is not particularly long-lasting. An eternal and more powerful union can never be attained as long as one is preoccupied with pursuing joy through a physical union. There is a deeper and more profound level of experience that teaches couples what it means to be a man or a woman. When two people realize that they are more than bodies, then they can become one at a deeper and richer level. A couple can attain a state of wisdom and happiness through a physical union by realizing that they are not united solely on this level, and learn to become aware of each other's deeper existence. People do not exist because their bodies exist; people exist because their essential nature *is* existence. The body's life and well-being depend upon this deeper existence.

Ultimately, if a couple becomes aware that the purpose of life lies beyond the level of physical pleasure or satisfaction, then their life together blooms like a flower. The flower of humanity will blossom forever on the day that couples truly understand this. If there is to be any wiser and more evolved society, it will originate in family life. This can be attained when men and women understand the deeper meaning of marriage and family.

CHAPTER 3

Children

Nature realized that two people living together might become bored eventually, and without another challenge, they might also become very selfish. So nature decided to create something special to help bind people together. Thus, a child comes and with the arrival of a child, a shared, common interest is born. Then nature begins to teach human beings to make many sacrifices for their children, and for their children's children, and finally, for the entire society.

It is an enormous responsibility to give birth to a child and to raise the child properly. When we appreciate the full importance of this experience, we can achieve a great joy and fulfillment in this process. To a woman, having a child is an especially important event. A woman doesn't want to remain merely a wife, but wants to become a mother as well. This is important to her at a very deep level.

As with everything that is important in life, a couple should prepare for the role of parenting. When a couple understands the significance of the process they are undertaking, and they have the maturity to be unselfish, then they are ready to have children. Many problems could be avoided if people did not have children until they understood and accepted this responsibility. Becoming a parent means learning to make sacrifices for the well-being of one's child. When immature and selfish people have children, they do much damage to their children and to the whole of society.

Parents should be aware of their motivations and expectations. Some people approach the process of parenthood with the expectation that children will fulfill their desires. For example, people may say, "I want to have a son but not a daughter," which means that their motivation is immature and selfish; they expect the child to satisfy their desires. Instead, potential parents should try to cultivate the attitude: "If the Lord wants me to serve someone as a parent, I will serve him or her, with all my might, all my heart, and all my mind. Whatever child God gives me, I will do my best to fulfill my duty toward that gift." If you want to make parenthood a spiritual path, learn to love and enjoy your parental duties. When you love your duties, then a deeper enjoyment of those duties will develop.

Sometimes, newly wedded couples conceive even though they have used contraceptives. This may cause a problem or crisis for them, because they were not yet fully prepared for such a surprise. In their confusion and shock, they may impart negative *samskaras*, or subtle mental and emotional impressions to the child. All children should be wanted children; it is a challenge to create this attitude. Perhaps for some months the wife considers aborting the baby, and then decides to have the child. In this emotional confusion, she may allow the child to be born, but neither of the parents may be fully prepared emotionally to bring up that child. Even in such difficult situations, the husband and wife can try to learn how to accept the situation and become good parents. As parents,

they have created a living being; God has used them as instruments to give birth to someone; this is meant to be a
joyful experience for them, but at first it may be a challenge to let go of their own expectations and plans.

Before a woman becomes pregnant or as soon as she
knows she is expecting a child, it is helpful if she considers
several important issues. She should examine the influence of all her activities and actions on the fetus she is carrying. She may decide that some changes are helpful in
making good physical, mental, and emotional prepara-
tions. Both parents should take an active role in considering what experiences are desirable and helpful during the
pregnancy. A wise woman will consider the types of food
she should eat, and even the kinds of literature and other
influences that are beneficial to her. Such thoughtful questions help both parents adjust to the new reality in their
life. During pregnancy, many traditional cultures recom-
mend that a mother-to-be should have pleasant, positive
entertainment, but avoid experiences or stimuli that are
ugly, frightening, or repulsive. Many women feel a desire
to avoid negativity, and try to create positive environments
for themselves. It is helpful if stress can be reduced in every possible way. Everyone should support this pregnancy
and try to provide a loving, happy environment.

A husband who is mature and sincere will realize that
his wife is carrying a child and needs love and support. Every day her face changes, and sometimes a man doesn't
fully understand this process. Sometimes an insecure husband becomes jealous and complains that his wife isn't
paying enough attention to him any more. He says to himself, "I thought married life was going to be full of joy, but
this pregnancy is a nuisance to me. She seems to be totally
preoccupied with the baby and doesn't pay enough attention to me."

In married life, there are three difficult stages during
which a relationship can break down. During those three

periods, if both partners are not aware of the changes taking place in themselves and their partners, both physically and in terms of the emotions and personality, then the marriage may be endangered.

One critical period occurs after the first seven years of marriage, when a significant biological and emotional change begins to take place in the partners, and they start to think differently. Unless they both consciously deepen their commitment to the marriage, problems can lead to damage in the relationship.

A second crucial period for both men and women occurs much later in life. Those who are knowledgeable understand what happens during the menopause period, in which a woman undergoes the change of life. This is a hard time for her, both physically and emotionally. A middle-aged man undergoes similar personality changes, and at times it may become difficult for either partner to cope with the other person during that period.

The birth of a child creates the third critical period that challenges both partners, although often this change takes place earlier in the relationship. A husband sometimes thinks that his wife is neglecting him. He thinks that she is paying more attention to the baby than to him, but if he wants to grow in his marriage he should not allow this attitude to develop or to remain in place. From the very beginning, when his wife first conceives, a man should cultivate a special attitude toward his partner. This means he treats her as a mother, with consideration and respect, and tries to appreciate and respect the changes that are taking place in her life. A woman also realizes that her life is changing; she is no longer only a wife, but is becoming a mother as well.

Both partners must prepare themselves emotionally and mentally for the responsibility of raising a child. It is helpful if they discuss the changes taking place. But that new stage of life is not a cause for worry. When they know they are becoming parents, some people worry needlessly, "What will happen to my child if I lose my job?" When people resolve this issue, they can be free from such worries. As much as possible, both parents can cultivate the attitude of pleasant-mindedness and contentment with the new phase of life.

Throughout our lives, we should certainly understand our duties and learn to do them well, but there is no need to create worry. When I was born, my mother did not have to worry or make conscious plans, but she had breasts full of milk and she fed me without any hesitation. Who made this arrangement? Who arranges to protect the chicken inside the eggshell? Who arranges for a child to remain protected in the womb of its mother? In the midst of such a miracle, the expectant mother can continue to work and do her duties pleasantly and cheerfully.

Many people feel burdened by their duties. They come to resent the responsibilities they have taken on and wish they were free of them. They continue to do these duties, but with a negative, unwilling attitude that makes them feel like slaves. Accept the duties of life and learn to do them with love; then these duties will not enslave you. A duty done without love creates a feeling of obligation. A man says, "Honey, I really don't want to do this, but I have to because you are my wife." If you do your duties with a disgusted, resentful feeling you will become tired and unhappy. Life will become a chore. That isn't the way to live joyfully; enjoying life means learning to accept and love your duties, so that those duties give you freedom and a sense of joy.

Often parents don't want to be completely available to their children, because they fear that the children will disturb their pleasures. Yet parents expect so much from their children and later complain that their children are distant and communicate poorly. Sincere fathers and mothers are willing and unafraid to make sacrifices for their children; that is a necessary part of being a parent. If parents want their children to grow and develop properly, they must learn to sacrifice and forego some of their personal interests for a higher purpose.

Children learn and develop appropriately when parents share themselves with their children, not when parents are selfish or possessive. Thinking first of the children's needs begins from the earliest moment; it influences every choice a parent makes. Sometimes a woman may worry that her figure will be spoiled if she nurses her child, or her doctor may tell her not to nurse the children because she will age earlier, or perhaps her husband says, "Don't nurse the child because then you won't look so attractive." Healthy mothers should breastfeed their children; it is the best and healthiest thing for a child. The father should be supportive of this process, and try to be patient and helpful to his wife during this time, rather than feeling that he is being neglected.

Some years ago, it became fashionable to try to feed children on a rigid schedule. This isn't helpful; when the baby needs food, he or she will cry for it. Although crying doesn't always indicate hunger, a mother can learn to recognize the different cries her baby makes. When a baby is fast asleep, it does not need to be awakened for a feeding. I have seen mothers who woke their babies just to make them eat. Once, I stayed for two months with a family that had a new baby. They had been told to feed their baby at exactly two o'clock every day. "Get up, baby, get up. I have to feed you," the mother would say as she disturbed the poor baby's sleep. Of course, the baby began to scream and the mother then forced the child to eat. In that upset state, it wasn't possible for the baby to eat or digest the food. One day I asked her, "Who told you to do this?"

She said, "My doctor told me to feed the baby on a schedule, every three hours."

I asked, "But did he tell you to disturb the baby even

when he is fast asleep?" I suggested that she telephone her doctor and describe what she was doing. The doctor explained that he had never meant to wake the child, but only to feed him about every three hours. Eventually, the problem was resolved and the poor baby could sleep when it needed to.

Almost all parents make a few foolish mistakes with their first baby, while they are learning to care for the child. Once I visited a home and the young mother was feeding her baby. After feeding him she immediately placed him in the crib and started to sing him a song, but the baby was restless because he had gas inside his stomach. I said, "Please hug and cuddle your baby. Do you hug your baby after a feeding?"

She answered, "No, but we love him very much!"

I said, "After you feed him, lift him up and just hug him, and then he will burp." I could tell from watching the baby that he was uncomfortable and restless, even though I had never raised a child myself.

So the mother picked up the baby and hugged him and when the gas in his stomach was expelled, he quickly fell asleep. The mother was amazed at my suggestion, but I was only observing the baby attentively. Mothers can learn to sense their child's needs and to communicate with the child silently, using "the language of silence."

People sometimes debate about which language is the mother of all languages—Sanskrit, Hebrew, or Latin—but actually the original language is the language in which a newborn baby speaks with its mother—by cooing, the language of love. The mother and baby coo and murmur wordlessly to each other. This is the mother of all languages. If you have such a wordless love for your child, rather than the mere feeling of having to do your duty, then your love will always help you carry out your role properly and you will do your best at meeting your child's needs.

There is an old Sanskrit axiom: *Ladeyet pancha varshani,* which means, "Love your child without limitation up to the age of five, and then begin to discipline him." Love your child without any reservations, and sacrifice your other pleasures for the sake of this love. Don't underestimate how early this sense of love is perceived; a child perceives your love before any other awareness.

Sometimes, when a baby is born, the modern doctor tells the couple from the beginning, "Don't allow your child to sleep in your bed, because it will disturb your sleep and your husband's sleep." The modern advice is that the baby's bedroom should be separate. But in applying this philosophy, the child may be ignored in some ways from the very beginning. In the modern style of parenting, neither the mother nor the father is as close to the children as they should be. Is this why many modern children don't love and respect their parents? Is it because parents have remained selfish and remote from the very beginning?

Some years ago I had an experience that was very shocking to me, and which made me wonder about the origins of many social problems. I was visiting the family of a medical doctor in New York State, and as we were finishing our visit, the hospital called to say that one of the hospital patients had suddenly died. The doctor telephoned the patient's only son to tell him the sad news. But when the man answered the phone, he told the physician, "Sorry, doctor, I don't have time to talk to you. I'm going to Florida on vacation with my girlfriend. I'll send you a check when I get back." And he hung up.

The doctor was speechless and I was astonished. I told the doctor I had to see that son, because I wondered what such a person was like. So he humored me and drove to the young man's address. We knocked on the door and he answered it with a suitcase in his hand. Behind him, his girlfriend was crying.

I told him, "I have to talk to you. I want to understand: your father has just died and you are going to Miami to enjoy a vacation with your girlfriend?"

The son replied coolly, "Yes, why not? My father never cared for me and I don't care for him. So now he is dead; what can I do? I'll send flowers to the funeral."

I could not convince him to stay, but his weeping girlfriend followed us to the car. "If this is how he treats his father, I'm going to leave him now. I don't want to marry such a man!" I didn't say anything, but I thought that perhaps she was making a good decision.

In the East—especially in Japan, India and China—parents were traditionally given great respect and devotion in the families; the mother and father were respected as wise teachers. In such a culture, no one would put a sick parent in a nursing home to die alone, but perhaps these parents also showed more attention to their children. Sometimes in the East, there is another problem: children have such respect for parents they cannot speak candidly or openly to them, which is also not helpful, but the breakdown of respect between parents and children in the West has occurred because parents don't respect and honor the importance of their own role in their children's lives.

I am a swami, and a swami is one who has burned all his worldly desires and relationships in the fire of knowledge. Because of this, I am not allowed to bow to or honor any worldly authority, even my father or mother. But if my mother came to me today and said, "You must jump in the ocean right now," I would not hesitate or question her, because of my respect for her role in my life. She took such pains in my upbringing, even though she lived for only a short time. How could anyone forget his mother's love for him? When children are given such care and love, then they will definitely learn to accept discipline. They will understand your love and respond to it. The seeds of love are sown very early in childhood.

In the meditative tradition, we say that a person on the spiritual path has three gurus. The word *guru* means "darkness dispeller," and when we discuss the role of the mother in a person's spiritual life we say, *"matri devo bhava,"* meaning "the mother is the first bright, shining being" in a person's life.

In the modern world we have come to take this role for granted, but what a mother experiences as she carries a child, experiences childbirth, and provides for it during the first years of its life, no one can ever fully understand. No matter how much a father loves his child, he cannot bestow this gift nor fully understand this love. The traditional view was that a person owes a debt of gratitude toward his or her mother for giving the gift of life. The call of the mother is the highest calling—it is a position of total selflessness—she loves unconditionally and without limits.

Later, after the mother has established this level of love and acceptance, the father plays his role, which also requires unselfish attention to the child. But no matter what modern people say, the roles of these two kinds of love are completely different. A father does so much for his child—he protects and supports the child in so many ways—but it is a different quality than maternal love. A child asks his father for spending money and the father says, "How much do you need? What will you spend it on?" This is a different role: a child needs discipline, too, or he or she cannot develop fully. But when a mother is nursing her newborn child she never thinks, "How much do you need?" She gives everything she can, and then allows the child to nurse on the other side as well. These two important roles are two ways of loving, and if the parents play their roles skillfully, then the child becomes capable of loving and being loved.

Human love is the most ancient traveler in the world. If one studies the nature of love, he or she will understand the way that human love shifts and moves across the course of life, as it evolves from one object to another. Love has been traveling since the beginning of time, but rarely does it achieve its final goal, the capacity to love all.

When a child is born, he first loves his mother's bosom, and she becomes the person who symbolizes love and security to him. Slowly that love is channeled toward dolls and toys. At this stage, children become hurt or angry if someone takes or destroys their toys, just as adults are angered if someone damages their possessions. Later, a child's attachments and attractions shift to other objects, and then, still later, to girl or boy friends, evolving all the time into the desire to own something to satisfy the ego. But the full reality of love is still far away, for the question remains: What is the purpose of life?

I once knew a wise and loving mother who spent time teaching her children every night when they were going to bed. She would gently remind them to say to themselves, "I am strong and I am not afraid of anything, because I love all and hate none. The purpose of my life is to serve, help, and love others."

Her children, who were raised in that environment and with that awareness, became great people because they learned to serve society. Their lives were examples for all. Unless we learn to become aware of others and sensitive to them, we can never really develop fully as human beings. This process begins with developing sensitivity toward those who live near us, in our families or with those in the same environment.

Often, parents make a serious mistake in raising their children. Instead of imparting a genuine education and understanding, they teach only the skill of imitation: "If I walk like this, or if I talk like this, you should also walk or talk like that." We teach children such imitative behaviors in the name of manners or etiquette, but childhood is meant to be a period of creative discovery;

imitation is only a small part of it.

Sometimes, young children are blamed for being destructive or breaking things. The parents may value a beautiful vase, but the child hasn't yet learned to appreciate its value, so he accidentally breaks the vase while playing. Rather than thinking of such a child as destructive and punishing the child severely, you must realize that your goal is to prevent such future behavior by teaching a child to understand and be sensitive to how others feel. Children need to learn this lesson to mature and become responsible and considerate of others. You teach a child to respect others and become sensitive to others by demonstrating that in your own behavior and then helping a child to be aware of others' feelings.

Instead, parents sometimes spank children, scolding them or telling them not to do things, but the children don't understand what their parents mean. If the parents lose their patience and use physical or verbal force on a child, they exert the force of their personality like a kind of violence directed against the child.

When parents exert force to control children, they suppress children's first hesitant efforts to explore and learn. Then the children's curiosity, which is the most basic quality necessary for their learning, may also be suppressed or killed. A deep pattern of repression and suppression can be created in the child's personality.

When a suppressed atmosphere is created, children react to this parental force or violence, and want to do things to get back at their parents. A child thinks, "When I grow up, I'll show them!" With this rebellious, negative attitude, they become even more destructive. It is not healthy to force children to imitate adults without helping children develop an understanding of *why* they should behave in a particular way. If children are to grow and develop fully, this sense of suppression or force must be avoided both at home and in the classroom.

Children become the fathers and mothers of the next generation of our society, so our society should provide all children with a complete education in how to be a healthy human being. Children should never be treated cruelly or harshly in the process of being educated. The whole essence of discipline is wrapped inside a small truth called love. If you really love your children and tell them not to do something, they will rarely misbehave. But if you bribe children with candy or presents and say, "I'll give you sweets if you don't do this," children will learn to demand bribes as a way of life, and that will be disastrous for the children and the entire family.

A common problem in parenting is that no matter how great and skilled we adults are at lying, we don't want our children to lie to us! We threaten, "Don't lie to me or I will spank you!" But the child thinks, "Mother lies to father and father lies to mother, so why shouldn't I lie?" Parents tell children to speak the truth, but children rarely understand these words, because they have seldom observed truth in the behavior of adults. In such an environment, how can children learn to depend upon and trust their parents? How can they learn to honor and give respect to their parents? Parents must first teach children the meaning of truth by demonstrating it in their own behavior.

Once, I was staying with a military officer and his family in Delhi. In the evening he said, "Swami, my children are going to bed at ten o'clock. Then my wife and I will quietly go to a movie, and the children won't know it."

I said, "I assure you, I won't tell them, but that's not the right way to behave. Your children will know you have deceived them."

The children pretended they were asleep, but the moment that the officer and his wife went out, they got up and said, "Uncle Swami, let's shout at the top of our voices."

I asked them why they wanted to shout and make noise.

They said, "When our parents drink they shout, but when we want to play and shout, they don't allow us to do that; they spank us. We want to shout—please help us! Let's have fun!"

I took them up on the roof, and I started shouting along with them. The whole neighborhood was amazed. Many officers gathered in front of the house. They noticed me standing on the roof, shouting with four children at ten o'clock at night! They asked, "Who are you and what are you doing?"

I said, "Look, I am playing with these children; why don't you go play with yours? What do you adults go to the movies to see? You go to hear and enjoy the excitement—shouting, screaming, and laughing—that's what we are doing here. The children simply want exactly what you want."

The point is that children will want to do what they see adults do, and being hypocritical with children usually causes rebelliousness. Sometimes, adults don't provide children with healthy examples. This absence of good role models or examples is one of the greatest deficiencies in childhood education, and it is what spawns the need for more police in our society. Parents are the prime examples for their children, and their behavior sets a course for children's entire lives. Consequently, parents should learn to be self-disciplined in their own speech and behavior as they bring up their children, since their children will learn from observing what the parents do, far more than from what they preach.

Children can also teach their parents, if the parents are prepared to learn. A parent can learn many things from children that can't be learned from books. The natural, honest way that children ask questions and their curiosity and eagerness to learn about things can be a good example for adults. Children notice new things about the world every day because they have a sense of curiosity;

they constantly want their parents to explain life to them. If parents spank a child, it may stop or suppress the child's observable behavior, but inside, the child grows resentful and may eventually destroy things. Many childhood problems are created in this manner. Parents expect children to become good citizens, but the children grow up influenced by adult behavior and mistakes. It is vital for mothers and fathers to realize how much their children will learn from their examples.

A great writer once said that a child should be educated twenty years before his birth. This means that the mother of a child should receive a good education, in preparation for the role of raising her children. If the mother doesn't understand her duties toward her children, or if both parents don't understand the necessity of sacrificing their personal pleasures for the sake of their children, then children will grow up, but in a wild, uncontrolled way that damages society. Much of the unrest and violence in the modern world is because some parents bring children into the world dishonestly. The parents are not genuinely willing to provide the constant love, attention, and selfless guidance that children need. Children who are deprived of this are usually either insecure or angry because they feel cheated of the love they deserve.

In later childhood and adolescence, such children create disturbances for themselves and others without understanding the source of these disturbances. In adult life, psychiatrists or therapists may try to comfort these adults or moderate the negative influences of their childhood, but the root cause of such problems still requires society's attention. We rest our hopes on the type of education that is imparted by colleges and universities, but the real ground for education is the home. Why do we not emphasize the health and emotional development of children in the first crucial years of their lives?

Parents sometimes think that if they do not express

their negative attitudes aloud to their children, the children will not know what is going on, but such parents are fooling themselves. Even if children are asleep at night when the parents are discussing something, the children can receive an awareness of these impressions while asleep or dreaming. Experiments have been done on this in some research centers in Europe. In one experiment that was repeated with a number of families, a child was allowed to sleep deeply. His parents began to argue and the child began to dream, but his sleep was disturbed and his dreams became frightening and did not allow the child to rest.

When parents disagree violently or when they are hostile to each other mentally, their negative thoughts disturb the children. Children are extremely sensitive to the emotions and thoughts of those around them. Many people naively think that children are not affected by adult thoughts and emotions, but children are highly sensitive to these adult psychological influences.

Compared with the power of our thoughts, the effects of our physical actions are insignificant. Only a small number of our thoughts are expressed in actions; actions themselves are nothing but extended thoughts. Because children are so close to us emotionally, they often receive our thoughts and are influenced by them. Children are not yet fully preoccupied with and attentive to the external environment, so they unconsciously receive our thoughts. In the modern world, scientists are not yet prepared to accept this truth; many will think that this is a ridiculous idea, but the day will come when scientists will understand and recognize that children are affected more by the thoughts and emotions of their parents and family members than by anything else in their environment.

The language of silence affects us all at the unconscious level. Children are very sensitive to this level of influence. If the parents are in conflict, or if their relationship is not loving and harmonious, they influence their children unconsciously, since children are a part of their parents. When parents experience emotional problems, their fears, confusions, and conflicts affect their children. Parents can learn to be aware of how their problems influence their children, and should be careful that they do not harm their children by the thoughts and emotions they cultivate.

Children unconsciously retain many ideas or impressions from what their parents say. During my childhood I received many impressions that way. I was sometimes very naughty; I used to run here and there and sometimes my guardians couldn't control me. To try to control my behavior, some adults would say, "A ghost lives under that tree. If you go over to that part of the garden, he will get you!" I was a very curious child, and I wanted to see the ghost, so I would go there to investigate, but I found nothing. I thought, "These adults are lying; I have never seen a ghost here!" But despite my own experiences, whenever I see a particular type of tree, even now as an adult, I recall their words. I am not afraid of ghosts, but the memory of their words returns when I see such a tree.

Many parents unknowingly plant seeds of weakness during the tender years of early childhood, and the child grows up with those weaknesses. But if parents realize that they have an opportunity to shape their children's lives and to guide the children from one path to another, they can take advantage of the creative opportunity to help their children develop.

Some children become rebellious, stubborn or deceitful because they don't receive enough love and attention from their parents. They yearn for parental attention and when they don't receive it, they become destructive. I remember how much I wanted attention as a child. My Master, who raised me from the age of three, used to sit in deep meditation for a long time, but I was a child and I wanted his attention, so I would break glasses. When he heard the noise, he would open his eyes and look at me and say, "Hey, what are you doing?!" And that attention was sufficient for me for a while. I wanted a reaction; I wanted somebody to notice what I was doing. I used to knowingly cause a commotion just so someone would notice that I existed.

All children do the same thing; if parents love one child more than the other children, or have a preference or give unequal attention to one child, then jealousy, competition, and many other emotional problems are created. Children compete against one another for attention, and the family is divided. Even when parents share their love fully with their children, problems may be caused by a lack of acceptance from the child's teachers in school or by other children. It is equally important that those who teach children love and accept them.

Many years ago, I was appointed by one of the Indian states to survey the educational problems of its children. I observed many children and their teachers. I discovered that many of the children's problems were related to their mothers, fathers, or teachers. When a teacher discriminated by showing a preference for certain children in class, or seemed to dislike or like particular children, it caused many problems. I noticed that teachers often released their own frustrations on the children. If a teacher's boyfriend or husband had mistreated her, she would come to school and upset the children.

Parents should realize that children can be very much influenced by interactions with others at school or elsewhere. They are often puzzled by a teacher's remarks about their children. "Your child is destructive; he or she does not know how to behave properly." If you receive such a report from a teacher, go and observe how the teacher is interacting with the child and how the child is being treated. Children are only children; they need to be trained, but they should always be treated with affection and respect.

Children reach an age when they understand how they ought to behave; they know right and wrong. Children know if their parents love them and sincerely want them to grow. When they know they are loved, they can be taught self-discipline. But if they observe that their parents are selfish or dishonest with them, they will imitate that negative behavior. Parents sometimes reap the fruits of this karma for a long time. It is the source of many later problems, particularly during adolescence. If adults smoke, drink or fail to behave responsibly, how will the children learn self-discipline and self-control?

Before you decide to have children, make a resolve: "We will sacrifice our joys and pleasures for the sake of our children. Whatever children God gives us, we will look after them with all of our hearts and with all our skill." When parents learn how to love and give to their children, then the children grow and develop to their full potential. But when the parents are selfish, children do not develop properly—they learn these selfish habits from their parents.

If we want to have a healthy society, then we should try to create a culture in which people appreciate the role of parenthood and approach the responsibilities realistically, understanding the need to prepare themselves for this great challenge. People would seek to learn patience, tolerance, self-discipline, and the ability to love and serve others before they sought to have children. It is very damaging for children to be raised by unprepared parents, who are still selfish and immature. I don't think anyone should have a child until he or she is fully prepared.

If people strengthen themselves and develop their selflessness in preparation for having children, then they can contribute healthy children to society. When people begin to think about becoming parents, and desire to have a child, they should understand the challenge and ask themselves, "Do I really deserve to have a child? Do I have the ability to care for the child materially, mentally, and emotionally? Do I have the capacity to raise a child selflessly?"

It is a great joy and benefit to have children, because raising children teaches parents sacrifice, self-discipline, love, and selfless service. Parents must renounce many joys for the sake of their children. Sometimes, for example, parents may want to go out for the evening, but once they become parents, they cannot always do what they want, because perhaps the children are ill or are about to arrive home from school, or there are other responsibilities the father or mother must carry out.

Having children and learning to sacrifice for their children can be particularly helpful to men. By facing and accepting such responsibilities, a man's selfishness can be curbed. He may decide to become less selfish because he loves and cares for his child. Slowly then, this fatherly love expands and extends itself to other children, to friends, neighbors, and eventually toward other people in society. But in the first step, you develop your selfless love for your own child. Charity always begins at home; in the home an adult can observe how selfish he really is and begin to correct and train himself.

Sometimes in the modern world, fathers return home from work late at night and leave most of the work of teaching children to their wives. Some children never see their fathers! It is important that fathers be involved closely in their children's development. Children crave this attention, and if the father neglects his role, the children will suffer, especially if they are sons. During infancy, the mother's efforts are most necessary, but as children develop, it is not helpful for children to have contact with only one parent. Parents should learn to be a skilled and loving team, supporting each other and working together to raise healthy children. Both fathers and mothers should demonstrate respect for each other so that children learn to respect them as well. When children observe parental conflicts they sometimes begin to treat their parents without respect.

In cases of divorce it is especially important for the parents to realize that they must cooperate and communicate effectively to avoid damaging their children. Children should never be "used" by parents in a competition to win love or respect. Sometimes fathers abandon their children, which can have disastrous consequences for the child's entire life. Adults must confront this selfishness in their own personalities, resolving to each other: "Even if we are not partners, we have a duty to our children. Let us not damage our innocent children with our selfishness or immaturity. Let us fulfill our responsibility with love and sincerity."

In many ways, children are a great joy. Children teach their parents many things. They teach them one of the greatest lessons in life: the capacity to love. Those who have children understand God's love. Those who don't have children can never quite experience this level of love. Through the process of raising children, adults can learn a higher level of love, a love that is unconditional and unselfish, and achieve a state of harmony and unity with the highest consciousness.

CHAPTER 4

The Stages of a Child's Growth

Welcoming a New Infant

The birth of a child provides great joy for a married couple, as well as an opportunity to come together even more closely through the shared interest in raising a healthy child. Children are born into a family, grow up in it, and are subject to all its influences—both those that thwart and those that shape growth. The training of any child begins in the family. The experiences that children have, particularly during infancy, leave deep-rooted impressions, because children are so open to these new learning experiences. If the family environment is healthy and beneficial for children, it helps them grow, for childhood is the foundation of adult maturity. The family can be a source of security and growth or conflict and difficulty, depending on how the infant is received.

Some couples today do not understand the pleasant

responsibilities of parenthood, and give birth to children without adequate emotional or mental preparation. It is good to have children, for raising children can teach parents that life is not meant solely for their own enjoyment—life is also a chance to love others. When parents raise children with this awareness, it helps expand the joy and consciousness of all family members, who are then able to share the love of their family with the community outside the home.

Unwanted and unloved children often lack vitality and zest for living. As infants, they may not thrive or grow; they become apathetic and withdrawn. Later, as young children, they feel insecure and suffer from stress and anxiety. Unloved children become hopeless, depressed, and passive. Their strength and physical and mental health are not sufficient to allow them to cope with their environment or develop their intellectual, social, or physical capacities. A child who is not nourished by love can never be nourished by food alone. Children who are kept in institutions and are deprived of the experience of parental love often present this same picture. It is essential for a young child to be in close contact with an attentive, loving mother for physical and mental well-being.

One of the most important principles of family life is that both parents should be prepared for the task of raising children, mentally, physically, emotionally, and spiritually. This ability to accept parenthood with contentment is very important, especially for the mother, because the role that a woman plays in raising children is quite different from the role she plays in any other area of life, socially or in her work. This role is special and very powerful.

An infant begins life completely dependent upon the blood and nourishment of its mother; its life is created by its parents and supported by its mother, without any effort of its own. As long as the child remains within the mother's womb, it is influenced by everything that affects her, and the child acquires certain subtle tendencies based on the actions, habits, thought patterns, emotions, and desires of the mother.

But even though a developing child is influenced by the habits of the mother during pregnancy, a child is also always an individual. If you observe a child—even a small infant—with sensitivity and attention, you will notice that the child is a subtle composite of its own independent qualities, plus the habits and tendencies of the mother and father. Thus, we need to appreciate both how much parental influences contribute to children's development, and how unique children are as individuals.

From the first days of an infant's life, and later, when a child is sick, distressed, or has been exposed to stress or harsh stimuli, there are simple, natural ways of treating an infant that will soothe and comfort the child. The parents' simple physical presence is reassuring. Feeding the infant promptly when it is hungry and making the baby as comfortable as possible are also very important. When the mother and father provide these forms of attention babies develop a sense of safety and security.

An infant receives its first experiences in life within the family, in its interactions with its parents. The impressions of the training that children receive in childhood are very deep-rooted, and children carry them throughout their lives. Small children learn quickly and form strong associations because their minds are not preoccupied.

After a child is born, it comes home into a new environment. A child's first conflicts with the world may be created when someone attempts to restrain or restrict its movement or attempts to impose a schedule on its needs. Another conflict arises later when a child is weaned from its mother's breast and deprived of the pleasures of sucking, and when a child is taught to eat new kinds of foods. Still later, conflicts arise when adults start to teach children to control the processes of elimination.

As infants develop and enter each successive stage, their curiosity leads them to investigate the surrounding world more fully. They receive different impressions from those around them. For example, close family members may handle an infant differently and suggest that the child behave in a variety of new ways. Infants are conditioned to love their mothers and fathers because of the close positive association that is created in daily life when parents provide comfort and help children satisfy their needs. Good parents do many things that allow children to feel safe and comfortable.

Parents' facial expressions, words, and the other ways of interacting with their children also have very powerful effects. Parents reward and share affection by hugging and kissing children; they punish children by depriving them of various things they want or raising their voices. These parental behaviors have a powerful impact, especially punishments, which come as shocks. As a result, children develop both love and hatred toward their parents.

Toddlers

Small children often find themselves restricted, for they are moved around, picked up, and controlled by everyone. Yet young children cannot control or dominate anyone themselves. Later, as children grow older and become stronger, they gain more freedom according to their readiness, but still, not all their demands are fulfilled; their real goal is to be transformed from a helpless infant to a powerful, self-managing adult. From infancy on, children want to assert self-reliance and become independent. Every individual desires this status; the ability to freely gratify all our desires requires that we achieve independence, yet there are many factors that prevent this transformation from occurring.

Sometimes parents try to resolve their confusion about how to raise children by operating from a rigid, inflexible point of view. They develop rules or policies but do not consider how these approaches affect the child. Sometimes, parents demand that children demonstrate obedience without question. Other times, parents make all their children's decisions for them or fight all of the children's battles. They sometimes do not understand the importance of the continuous process through which the child becomes an increasingly independent individual. Some parents don't have the patience or willingness to take the time required to understand what infants or toddlers want or help children learn to do things for themselves.

There is an old saying that the parents of a first child foolishly think that the child is a living doll or toy, who exists merely to fulfill their personal desire to "own" someone. This sense of "ownership" is sensed by children and it causes resentment. Parental possessiveness contributes to a child's growing feeling of resistance to being controlled and a desire for increasing independence. Parents sometimes want a toddler to remain little, helpless, and dependent, because it builds their egos and makes them feel important and superior. They unknowingly use the child as an object of their love, and try to keep the child dependent and bound to them as long as possible. Sometimes they keep the child close to them at home and do not allow the child's environment to expand. A healthy child wants to increasingly explore more and more of the world.

Children may become the victims of parental behavior that promotes dependency and become reconciled to this treatment because in some ways, dependency is comfortable and pleasurable for them. Such children become passive and insecure, and remain dependent. They feel secure only as long as they do not have to leave their parental homes. For example, when they reach school age, they may become fearful and withdrawn. These emotional disturbances created early in life can become major obstacles in the growth of the child, and can later interfere with the process of becoming an independent adult. When a young person encounters the many demands and complexities that are a part of adult life and love, he or she may find it difficult to adjust. Some young adults become so dependent that when they try to adjust to an independent life they lose their emotional equilibrium and become disturbed.

Before children leave the first training ground of the home to attend school, they have also learned a set of standards and principles about how they are expected to interact with others. This set of principles creates a powerful influence on the child's personality.

A new phase of life begins when children go to school. Now they must learn to adjust to the standards they encounter in the environment outside the home. They must learn to skillfully apply and integrate these two sets of values. Parents often have set habits of thinking or understanding; they are more conservative and rigid in their ways of operating than are children. Young children may have to cope with a strict code of conduct in the home, and yet must learn to adapt to the changing world outside the home with its new experiences.

This is a particular problem for children who are raised in the West by parents who are from the East. There may be two conflicting sets of values and standards—in the home and outside. Sometimes, this may create a major conflict and emotional crisis for children. Often, the source of the problem is that the parents themselves have not yet fully resolved the problem of how to live skillfully in two cultures. Sometimes parents adopt materialistic values themselves, yet expect their children to retain traditional patterns of behavior. To help a child deal with such different patterns and sets of values, parents must be honest and avoid hypocrisy in the behaviors they demonstrate.

The education imparted to children at home during childhood becomes the foundation of their life as develop-

ing individuals. Increasingly, the "environmental education" that children receive outside the home further influences the structure of their lives. In the modern world, the
gap between the home and the world outside the home is
likely to be wider than ever before. Sometimes parents exert excessive personal pressure on their children, trying to
mold a child's character according to their own way of
thinking and their cultural traditions. A parent can help a
child with such a situation if he or she is open and able to
listen to children express their feelings.

Attachments, Conflict, and Love

Throughout life, individuals go through many stages in
the development of their capacity to love. They grow by
learning new things and encountering new situations, but
their decision-making faculty may still remain immature. It
takes a long time for a person to learn to evaluate life's
experiences and recognize which experiences to take in
and which to avoid. Each experience helps a person to
strengthen his or her decisive faculty.

A small child loves or becomes attached to experiences
and objects because they stimulate the child's sensory re-
ceptors, satisfy his or her desires, or provide pleasure and
relieve tensions. Small children constantly experience the
ups and downs of trying to gratify their senses, encountering many frustrations in the process, which become the
cause of conflict and stress.

Children cannot always immediately attain the pleasures they desire, which causes frustration, as when a child
is hungry, cold, tired, or seeks reassurance. This is one of
the basic conflicts in a child's life. The resulting sense of
frustration and powerlessness leads to fear and anger.

A growing infant first "loves" itself and thinks of itself
in a self-centered way, believing that all the objects in the
home or world outside the home exist only for its enjoyment. Children learn to arouse and prolong pleasure by

stimulating their sensitive zones. For example, they do this by sucking, chewing or touching objects. This tendency to self-gratification exists in all children, yet if this theme of self-gratification becomes too well-established, children may become preoccupied with themselves and with satisfying their own desires throughout life. Later, this may make it difficult or impossible for them to form the love attachment to other individuals.

If young children build boundaries around themselves by gratifying their own senses, they do not learn to become aware of the obstacles and conflicts they create when their interests clash with those of others. It is important that children learn to be attentive to the needs, feelings, and desires of others too, or they can never mature as human beings. During these early years, children need to learn to share. This is a difficult time, when a child needs skilled, loving, and fair guidance, but children sometimes encounter a generation gap between their own thinking and that of their parents. Often children are left to their own resources in their attempts to explore the possibility of experiencing constant happiness. Adults usually do not teach children how to integrate this motivation to please themselves with an awareness of others' needs, because the parents themselves have often not learned to balance their desire for pleasure with a sensitivity to others.

As small children explore the external world, their ability to learn can be obstructed if they become obsessed with fulfilling their many changing desires. A craving to possess and enjoy objects begins to become even more intense. When such a desire or craving is forcibly inhibited by an opposing motive, like the fear of punishment, the processes of repression and suppression begin. Conflicts arise in the process of imparting moral training because children are taught to avoid acknowledging certain emotions, desires for particular pleasures, or tendencies that exist in themselves.

Unfortunately, children encounter many difficulties, for they are not yet aware that if the objects of joy and pleasure are meant for them to enjoy, these objects are also meant to give enjoyment to others. Children innately want to take but do not want to give or share. It is difficult for a child to learn to give, for initially, he or she has only formed the habit of taking. This strengthens the individual's ego and makes children self-involved, egotistical, and self-centered. A child becomes attached to the things he or she enjoys and calls them "mine." This is natural for children, yet to develop as healthy people, children must learn to share and not remain self-centered.

But love is the most ancient traveler in the universe, and the nature of love is to travel, evolve, and grow. After the first period of self-involvement and self-love, comes the next phase, the emergence of love for the parents. The mother becomes the first focus of this love, because she constantly attends to the child and to its needs. If a child receives this love, then a child enters the next phase, that of learning to share.

Parental Attachment

Love is the guiding force of life, but when love is mingled with attachment—which is pure selfishness—then attachment blinds those who want to love. There is no remedy for selfish "love." Selfish parental attachment is the worst barrier on the path of a child's growth, and it can do damage by thwarting a child's unique development.

Decades ago, Freud suggested that male children show a natural preference for their mother and female children show a preference for their father. He discovered this to be true when he started to deal with his adult patients. By tracing the development of their love lives back to early childhood, he found that many adults had not yet emerged from childhood. Parents probably unconsciously encourage these preferences on the part of their children, and they act without being aware of how they provide such encouragement.

Sometimes difficult or dangerous situations are created when widows are left with only sons after their husband's death. Because their emotional life is disrupted and their romantic love is thwarted in its expression, they sometimes use their male children unconsciously as partial substitutes for what they are lacking. This relationship of excessive attachment can become a stumbling block in the unfoldment of the child's life. Such mothers may later resent their sons' love for other women. These sons may experience great difficulty and guilt in sharing their love with wives or girlfriends; sometimes, they become dependent and yearn to return to the protecting arms of their mothers.

Other times, parents want to fulfill their own hidden, unfulfilled desires through their children. They may do this by expecting their child to succeed or be skilled in some particular area. They forget that healthy children need to be allowed to grow freely, so that their individual growth is not suppressed. It is very destructive when parents force their ideas, views, and suggestions on their children, either consciously or unconsciously. The goal of parenting is to help children become strong and independent, but we need to learn to guide them and not control or command them. It is a challenge for parents to create an environment that favors and promotes the independent growth of children. Harsh treatment, excessive criticism, rudeness, and frequent punishments can all damage children's personalities. Children are curious and want to understand the world; loving parents learn to channel this curiosity rather than hinder or suppress it.

Just as excessive parental love and attachment can be harmful, so also can insufficient attention and love. Many young parents who want to bring up their children according to modern child-rearing principles have heard of the dangers of parental attachment. Sometimes people go to the opposite extreme, and ignore or neglect the important learning period of childhood. Such children grow up independently, but in a negative way—they grow up without any love or discipline, and they often become selfish.

The ancient scriptures of the East provide some guidelines for parents. They teach that children need unconditional love and acceptance up to the age of five. From five to the age of ten, it is said that children need both love and discipline.

Good discipline is not damaging to the growth of a child, but it should not be imposed rigidly. We can teach children self-discipline in a gentle and loving manner. Children need love; those who have not been touched, held, kissed, hugged, and caressed become mute when they face the task of expressing their love later in life.

All over the world, violence in children is increasing. If we want to reverse this trend, we must help parents learn how to bring up children with love. The resentment, rebelliousness, and stubbornness that seem common in many young people are the result of the patterns that children learn in childhood, and are due to the violence or selfishness of their parents. Unfortunately, the home is often the source of negative training.

With loving, attentive guidance, all children can learn to care for themselves and interact positively with others. It has been discovered, for example, that many retarded children can become self-managing and responsible for themselves if they receive the proper guidance and good training. If we provide children with an educational environment and with affection and support, they can accept a course of education.

Parents who are selfish do not demonstrate love and self-discipline; they fail to serve as examples for their children. They can never make themselves happy, nor can they teach children to live successfully and happily. They transmit their selfishness to their children and these children further damage society.

It is important for parents to express affection and love for their children, so that children's natural cravings for love and affection are satisfied. Love is like food: if a child is malnourished, the child's body becomes weak; if the child is not given love, the child's "emotional body" becomes weak. The love children receive from their parents becomes the center from which they grow. This allows children to learn to radiate love outward to the whole universe. If parents are unable or unwilling to give children love and affection, then establishing a family is a very dangerous endeavor, which can have disastrous consequences, both for the family and for society as a whole.

Later Childhood and Adolescence

Between the ages of ten and eighteen, children need friendly guidance. Cravings, desires, and a need for emotional outlets are natural tendencies at this stage. If these desires are not fulfilled, children of this age start to substitute other desires for them. Some of these new desires are healthy and socially acceptable, while others are not.

During this stage of life, children start to explore many new things in the world outside the home and start to establish their place in society. As far as the development of creativity is concerned, this is the most important period in a person's life. Learning to paint, sing, play musical instruments or dance are all appropriate channels for children's desire to create and challenge themselves—and each of these processes help children learn self-discipline.

Among the many conflicts arising from the home and the environment outside the home, the most difficult conflicts are of a sexual nature. When children play with others in early childhood, they want to be with a group of their own gender. They have things in common that they want to share and they can gratify certain wishes, wants, and desires. In the beginning, boys and girls resent the intrusion of the opposite sex because of their close same-sex friendship circles.

Later, in group activities, boys and girls become curious and want to learn about each other. In this period, unfortunate attachments to individuals can occur. These attachments can cause difficulties because often there is no appropriate way for the attachment to be expressed or fulfilled. In modern society, there is a preoccupation with sexuality and pressure for children to be sexually aware at an early age. But children do not yet have the maturity to handle the feelings and tension created by this sexual pressure from society. Thus, a pattern develops that has an element of sexual play and sexual talk, with flirtatious behavior and increasing tension. This excitement jars and agitates children's nervous systems and becomes associated with the individuals whose thoughts, speech, and deeds arouse these reactions. The present social environment inevitably seems to create this tension and conflict.

In almost all cultures, the subject of sex has been one of the most powerful taboos. Parents often try to avoid this topic, especially in the East, which causes many problems. Both the pattern of suppressing emotions and that of expressing emotions without understanding their nature create great confusion for children.

Children and young people don't yet understand the importance of their relationships with the objects of the world and with other creatures. They have not yet developed the faculty of decisiveness—the ability to decide and judge things and to determine what is best for themselves. If parents express their emotions without self-control, then children do not learn to control their emotions or use their emotional power positively. Children need to be taught by a wise parent how to acknowledge and express emotions without either extreme of self-indulgence or suppression. Repression of emotions is dangerous; conscious control is very helpful to a person's development.

When cravings are not satisfied or dissipated, they persist or recur, seeking to find a new way of gaining their ends. If parents teach children to sharpen their inner faculty of decisiveness, helping them learn to be aware of their desires and how to manage them, children can learn to pacify themselves, sublimate their emotions, and direct and use the power of emotion creatively.

Children in the modern world need a type of education that helps them to understand their sexuality and the changes they experience. But children should also be taught what is injurious and what is not. Teenagers are becoming active sexually at younger ages, and this damages their health and spreads disease. It also damages them emotionally, because they are not mature enough to handle the pressures they receive from others. When they become attached to others who are not yet capable of mature relationships, their tender hearts are often shattered.

In the pressure to meet societal expectations, some older children and teenagers feel inadequate or incompetent, which damages their sense of self-esteem and leads to a deep sense of insecurity. Because of this, many boys and girls develop feelings of inadequacy and fear, and cannot have healthy relationships later in life.

But in order to help young people, adults need to examine the values that children are taught through the media and on television. Women are not respected in many parts of the world. In the West, for example, images of their bodies are used to sell objects and attract commercial attention. In the midst of this disrespect for women, how do adults expect children to learn to respect each other and have healthy attitudes about love and responsibility? Adults must avoid hypocrisy in their own behavior. Adolescents are very observant; if parents try to restrict children's freedom, but themselves watch television shows or movies that have violent or degrading themes, how can children learn to discipline themselves?

If adults want to help young people learn to have healthy sexual attitudes and behaviors, they must first learn to control their own sexuality, and learn to lovingly and responsibly express this positive force. Adults must begin to consider whether those who are greedy should be allowed to confuse and mislead children by selling sexual images and stimulation for a profit. Children are constantly bombarded by these stimuli, and they are unable to cope adequately with this agitation and arousal.

Disappointments and experiences that create frustrations for children cause them to become violent or destructive. Children should be taught to care for and express affection towards younger children, pets, and even plants or wild birds. Gardening, painting, music, sports, and other creative arts are also healthy pastimes, as well as the academic subjects taught in school.

This sort of emotional sublimation is helpful for children because it allows them to channel their energy positively. All emotions spring originally from the four primitive sources, and these cannot be ignored if we want children to develop in healthy ways. These four drives are the desires for food, sleep, sex, and self-preservation. Ideally, children should receive parental training and education in how to regulate and channel these four main appetites. They should be taught that if these appetites are not regulated and balanced, they can create physical and emotional disorders. But unfortunately, it is rare for parents to impart such training, because they themselves do not understand the four main appetites or how to skillfully and constructively channel them.

Many young people are well-fed, but are not taught how to become aware of their full potential. They may look well-built and well-nourished, but they do not know anything about the process of communication with others. The problem of human communication grows and changes with the development of a human being.

Constant, friendly guidance is essential for children, especially during puberty. Children should be taught to sublimate and channel their desires through socially accepted substitutes, so that they don't experience the many deep frustrations that seem to be personal in the beginning, but later become related to others.

Boys and girls develop a sense of loyalty to each other during early adolescence. They start to adore and admire each other. This is because of the inborn desire that all people have to surround themselves with friends. Sometimes in such relationships, an excessive attachment to certain individuals develops. Children easily form "crushes" and their tender and impressionable minds become active in a very one-pointed way. In such cases, because they are inexperienced and sensitive, they may become strongly conditioned to desire and love in a particular way, and an emotional habit may become established. If this conditioned pattern of love and attachment is unhealthy, they may fail to adjust to the process of adult love later in life.

When we carefully examine the basis of our emotions, we find that we are always related to someone in one way or another. When we learn this, a sense of consideration for others develops. This is the turning-point in a human life, when a child can either remain selfish and conceited or can become loving and gentle, capable of consideration for others.

Parents should not only observe their children's behavior during the waking state, but should also study the deeper aspects of children's minds by learning about their dreams and the things they imagine and fantasize about. Daydreams, fantasy, and imagination are natural, useful, and therapeutic pastimes if they do not become excessive. Sometimes, when they serve as substitutes or compensations for disappointments and frustrations that children cannot control, they are helpful in relieving some of children's tensions.

As children enter adolescence, their biochemistry changes, especially their hormone levels. Adult love habits are formed as this stage progresses. Some individuals cannot leave behind the strong attachments of childhood, even when puberty is reached. When an interest in the opposite sex begins to develop, some cannot accept and adjust to this naturally or allow their natural interests to develop, because their adolescent behaviors or desires have become conditioned in the direction of habitual masturbation or homosexuality. Sometimes adolescents lose confidence in themselves or think they will not be able to perform as adults or be accepted by others. This creates a powerful complex for them. Children do not suddenly develop love for the opposite sex; this attraction builds in their minds after they have observed adult romantic love for some time.

During adolescence, as they deal with their developing sexuality, young people need their parents to provide careful attention and friendship. Wise parents do not create distrust in their children, which happens when parents are not honest with their children, behave hypocritically, or do not listen to what their children are trying to express. When children do not trust their parents—who are supposed to be the child's best friends—then they often start to experiment on their own, sometimes misusing sexual practices and experiences for the sake of personal pleasure and joy. When parents lose the trust of their children, the children will no longer discuss their concerns and problems openly with them. Then the parents can no longer provide any guidance.

Habits are formed when a person repeats an action or behavior again and again. Habits create the child's character and eventually form the personality. Parents who understand the problems that can arise from the influences young people receive outside the home always spend time with their children, so that the children have confidence in them and trust their love and guidance.

The stage of adolescence is often difficult for both parents and children. When children complete this stage, they become more self-reliant and then they begin to think about leading their lives independently. Eventually, young people begin to think about marriage and start to look for a relationship that suits their social, mental, and emotional natures.

Raising Healthy Young People

It has been said that "the child is the father of the man," and this is true. It is also true that a healthy adult is not only a citizen of his or her own nation or country, but also a citizen of the world. Childhood is the architect and designer of the entire life, and it creates a blueprint for a person's development.

Children almost always identify themselves with their parents through the way they express love and hatred. Parents also identify with their children and attempt to gratify their unfulfilled desires through their children. For example, if a parent feels that he or she has married below his or her social status, that parent may pressure the children into social achievement. Sometimes a parent had an unfulfilled goal—perhaps he or she wanted to be a doctor, but was forced to choose a more modest job because of social pressures or circumstances. Such parents may subtly force their children to attain the profession the parent craved, rather than allow the child to express and pursue his or her own desires.

If parents understood what it means to train their children appropriately and learned how to do so, then our modern society would not continue to suffer from so many difficulties. Many modern social problems result from a lack of appropriate training in childhood. When people decide to have a child, there are two essential points they should consider. First, the parents themselves should become examples for the child, willing to help the child learn the principles of life and practice them every day. Second, parents should make a resolution not to remain selfish, but to accept the challenge of sacrificing their joys and pleasures for the sake of their children's growth.

Healthy children grow up assuming that nothing will interfere with or prevent their growth in life. They are taught to be self-reliant and confident, and their learning is encouraged rather than forced. Many children who have learning disabilities begin to learn when they are treated lovingly and are given an opportunity to express their talents. Every human being has potential, and if we know how to help children express that potential in creative ways, we can solve many problems in our society.

If children are taught how to spiritualize their actions, they can expand their awareness easily. Expansion of awareness leads a person to realize the unknown levels of life. Understanding all the levels of ourselves is the fulfillment of life's purpose. It is important to have a positive, creative aim in life. Awareness and sensitivity to ourselves and others are necessary to fulfill these goals.

Parents can teach children to create genuine stillness and become aware of other dimensions of their life, rather than scolding children to keep quiet. A human being is not only a body or a breathing being; a human being is also a thinking and feeling being.

When children are taught to become aware of their internal states from the very beginning, they can become creative and aware of deeper levels. Parents can teach children simple practices, including sitting quietly, paying attention to the breath, and practicing meditation. These help children strengthen their memory and sharpen their faculty of decisiveness. Children can become aware that the center of Consciousness is within themselves. When parents respect and honor this special presence in their children, children also learn to recognize and value it in themselves.

CHAPTER 5

Attaining Spiritual Fulfillment

The Journey of Love

If you study the evolution of love, you will realize that love is actually the oldest and most ancient traveler in the universe. Love has been traveling constantly, and it will continue to do so from eternity to eternity. Even before this earth came into existence, the omniscient and omnipotent power that you call Truth had expanded itself and expressed itself because of the power of love. Love itself means expansion, and its only opposite in the universe is the force of contraction and hatred.

As love travels, it goes through many phases in its expression; it changes and evolves on its way. A child is born and comes to the earth because love has journeyed along with two people, and as a result, love creates a child. If the relationship of love between a husband and wife was complete and limitless, they would not need a child, but their

87

love wants to evolve, so a child is born. No one needs to read a book to love a child; if you are a parent you have learned this already. Your son or daughter is born and you look at the child and you know that you love—and love has made another stop on its journey.

At first, the nature of a child's love is self-love—it appreciates only its own existence, and then slowly it comes to appreciate the existence of its mother, who feeds it. The child becomes attached to its mother and loves her in the way it is capable of at this stage. Love continues on its way; soon the child loves its father and then its love travels to other things—to dolls, toy animals, or other bright objects. Then the child begins to love and become attached to other children and adults, as well as to games and activities. The child's love travels on still further, to attractive clothes and then finally to a circle of friends. All along its journey, love lets go of some objects and attractions and moves on to others. As this happens, the child grows, matures, and becomes increasingly aware of the external world.

Finally the child becomes a young adult, and then love wants to find still another object for its attention. Love begins to move toward accomplishments and achievements, to many expressions of individuality. The love seeks a boyfriend or girlfriend, and finally love expresses itself in the choice of another person with whom to live one's life. All along the way, as consciousness has expanded, love has traveled on, choosing increasingly fine and special expressions.

Eventually, love comes in a circle; it travels on, seeking a child and the experience of parenthood. As long as love travels, we are learning and growing, but whenever we try to stop love in its travels, we create a pool of stagnation. We create this stagnation by refusing to love or become involved with others because we are afraid of outgrowing our selfishness and our attachments to our own pleasures.

We can also create stagnation if we start a family but live only for our own ego.

Whenever we do this, we are holding love back on its journey. Love is meant to grow and to increasingly radiate outward in ever-expanding and widening circles from the center within ourselves to the entire world. The whole purpose of a loving family life is to serve as a way station on this journey.

As love travels on its way it becomes increasingly powerful. In fact, love is the only force that can ever really change the world or help people to grow. The greatest kind of strength that a human being can have is the gentle strength of love. Once, many years ago, in my travels in the Himalayas, I went to see a sage living far away from anyone else. As evening approached he told me I should leave, because he needed to make dinner for his children, and I was very surprised to think that he had children there in the wilderness. But before I could leave I heard a low growl—the sound of tigers! I was somewhat alarmed until he explained that those were his "children." He had tamed two wild tigers with the force of his love, and they came every evening to take bread that he would make for them.

Love can tame all that is wild and uncontrolled; love is the only force that will help us end the violence and destruction in the world. Wherever we find young people who are growing up in a positive way, strong and self-confident, with the capacity to give to others and contribute to the world, we will recognize the effects of having been loved.

No one needs to learn to love; love is the natural capacity of human beings, if a person is not suppressed or constricted. Children will naturally develop the capacity to love and care for others, if their natural tendencies are allowed to be expressed. Certainly a person can learn to become negative and to hate, but that is not the natural pattern; it is a distortion. When we reach a certain stage in our development as human beings, we feel for others. Then, if someone else cries or is in pain, our hearts also feel their pain and we express our empathy. A person could be cold and cruel to another, but that is not the natural pattern.

Throughout life, love grows and matures, seeking its final fulfillment, the capacity to love all. When we have learned to love and eliminate all barriers, we achieve the highest state of consciousness.

Marriage and Spiritual Intimacy

In the marriage relationship, husbands and wives often become very close and interconnected physically, emotionally, socially and legally. But no matter how close a husband and wife are, if they have not completely understood the goals of marriage, then they cannot fully enjoy their relationship. They will never attain a true intimacy, but will instead develop a kind of dualistic personality with the other.

Many couples decide to live together with a type of material, worldly contract—they agree to raise children, own a house, and share their daily activities, such as visiting relatives. If they do not have any clearly formulated aim of their own in life, they may marry from a concern about other people's reactions and social expectations. Such people often live together for the sake of what others think of them. If this is the case, then something important is missing in the marriage, for such a couple has shared only the superficial aspects of life. However, when married people develop the awareness that their relationship is meant to help them attain the deeper purpose of life, they can create a complete mental, physical, emotional, and spiritual participation, and then the marriage can lead them to genuine fulfillment.

A couple should realize that just as they are one physically, emotionally, legally, and socially, they can also learn to become one spiritually. Achieving this inner oneness and unity is very important, because our outward behavior and interaction can't provide everything we are seeking. If two people live together physically, but never genuinely love each other on the deepest level, then within their conscious or unconscious minds there will always be conflicts or disturbances. If people live together without love, they hurt and cheat themselves and create confusion within. Throughout married life, two people should continuously seek to become genuinely and progressively closer and more intimate in their relationship—mentally, emotionally, and spiritually.

There is a danger that all married couples face—the danger that they may eventually get fed up with each other and abandon the goal of working toward unity. This tendency affects not only the young, but also older people. Sometimes people live together, not because they actually want to live together or maintain the relationship, but because they think they cannot live any other way; they have become dependent upon each other, and no longer have confidence in their own strength.

Some husbands and wives create a pattern in their marriage of using each other to vent or release their emotions. Perhaps the husband experiences problems at work and criticizes his wife, calling her names and letting out all his frustrations on her. Eventually, when she encounters problems, he receives the same treatment from her. If this process goes on for a long period of time, a feeling of bondage and resentment will replace their love. Then, instead of growing in love, understanding and acceptance, each partner becomes increasingly dependent upon the other.

If people have entered marriage thinking that their wife or husband will make them happy or that they will make their spouse happy, they have made a mistake. A mature person needs to outgrow such foolish and childlike ideas.

Each person must learn to be happy within himself or herself. This is the one truth everyone who marries should understand: happiness lies only within. Trying to find happiness outside oneself, by depending on another person's behavior, leads only to frustration, anger, and resentment. People expect too much from others, and when those expectations are not fulfilled, they lose their temper and become angry, injuring their nervous system and interfering with their mental clarity. This also further harms their relationship with the other person. It is only when people find happiness within that they can genuinely love and respect another. Paradoxically, it is a sense of individuality that allows for genuine closeness.

In the adjustment process that takes place between two people, respect and reverence for the other person are the first requirements, no matter how many disagreements or conflicting opinions there are. Married people always remain unique individuals. Their tastes are different; they feel and think differently. Consequently, both must have respect for their partner's individuality. Some people create unnecessary problems for themselves by trying to deny their partner's uniqueness. No matter what happens, a couple's inner connection of respect and acceptance should grow stronger every day.

The most important adjustment in marriage is the mental adjustment. The habit people have of judging others may be deeply rooted in each partner's personality. Unfortunately, when people are insecure and negative, they sometimes create conflict by condemning or criticizing their partners for minor habits that are different from their own expectations. Then, such people may seek happiness elsewhere, in a different relationship.

From a distance, everything and everyone seems to be exciting and glamorous. There is an old saying in India that reminds us that the drums that we hear in the distance sound fascinating, but when we examine a drum firsthand, we realize that it is hollow inside. Every person who marries should resolve not to be affected by the charms, temptations, and attractions of the external world. Resolve not to let these superficial attractions and temptations interfere with your marriage relationship. The world doesn't really offer anything of eternal value; actually, the world is full of obstacles. The challenge all married people face is to make their present situation a means to happiness. A relationship is not an obstacle to happiness—in fact, married life is meant as a means toward the goal of perennial happiness.

There is a verse in the scriptures that says, "Oh man, aspire to live for one hundred years." The desire to live for a hundred years isn't a bad goal; it is a fine desire, providing that your life has an aim or purpose. But it isn't healthy to live aimlessly, seeking only the pleasures of the senses. That kind of aimless, superficial approach doesn't ever lead to a long, meaningful life.

Understanding the purpose of life helps people live in a healthy way, for a long time. The duties of life—having children, dealing with society, and earning a living—are only steps in the process of life; none of these are the ultimate aim of human life. A couple doesn't remain together for the sole purpose of producing children. As wonderful as children are, having children isn't the highest aim in life; a child does not satisfy all the aspects of ourselves. After a couple has a child, they wonder, what next? Many people still don't know what is next; they are constantly searching for something more. They are looking for a deeper happiness.

All worldly attainments and achievements can be means to happiness, provided that a person knows how to use them. However, if people don't know how to use these opportunities wisely, they become obstacles. A marriage relationship can either create personal disaster or bring a great change for the better in a person's life. Through marriage and the process of learning to love, a whole personality can be changed and transformed, and a whole life can be remodeled toward happiness.

A couple should learn to enjoy themselves in all of the circumstances and situations of life. If a couple does not have a child, it doesn't matter; their attitude should be, "Because we do not have children we will devote more time to our spiritual practices and to the goal of enlightenment. We can also do many things to help the children of other families. In this way, we can enjoy life and attain fulfillment by helping others."

What is the purpose of life? A young person thinks, "I have to learn to support myself in the world," so the first twenty-five years of life are utilized for that. The second twenty-five years are used by men and women to understand the kind of relationship a man can offer a woman, and what a woman can offer a man. Unfortunately, what usually happens is that the more they offer each other, the more they need each other. They become excessively influenced by each other's personalities, and eventually develop an unhealthy dependence on each other. But marriage isn't meant to create dependence; this union is meant to help people attain a state of perennial happiness.

During the early period of marriage, from ages twenty-five to fifty, people often completely change their individual lifestyle, because they have others to consider. For example, the thought arises in a man's mind, "I would like to go to the club or to a movie," but then he thinks, "I have a wife and child; it is better for me to go home. I should be with my wife and child." A man can no longer live the way he did in his bachelor days, because in a bachelor's life there is little sharing or responsibility. But through marriage, people learn to share with each other; they share pain, pleasure, joy, and disappointments. Sharing involves a mental and emotional adjustment. Once a couple makes this adjustment, then the union guides in their mutual growth.

Actually, the second twenty-five years of life are often very difficult. Parents may call them years of enjoyment, but I consider them to be difficult and challenging years, in which parents have many responsibilities. They are concerned about their children's education and well-being, and they are also preparing for their own old age. Pressures come and go, and sometimes the partners develop fears that make them self-centered or even cruel or violent. This is because they have not yet learned to consider others; they only see themselves through the viewpoint of their increasing fear and insecurity.

This stage of life can become a time of greed, competition, and selfish discrimination. Society seems to foster this vicious pattern of living: we start to compare ourselves with others and then we become envious or jealous. Many of these reactions are caused by competition that results from our insecurities. A man or woman may become jealous and compete with another person's clothing, career successes or home. But no matter how much we achieve as we compete and strive to prove that we are better than others, we can never satisfy or eliminate this tendency in our own mind. The only way to lay to rest this driving insecurity is through a process of introspection, self-dialogue, and self-counseling.

Many people create this competitive jealousy within themselves, a jealousy even toward their wife or husband. But if their goal is to be happy, it is not helpful to imitate others or to compete with them. A more fulfilling and peaceful existence can be created if we learn to live simply and gently, and to cultivate pleasant, positive thoughts, rather than competitive states of mind.

If you want to resolve your insecurities, be realistic and practical: plan for the future; this means having a definite aim. Your desire to achieve your aims becomes stronger when you use your mind to make plans. The desire grows stronger and eventually you will realize it materially. Your desire for the goal helps give you strength from within. The more powerful your desire, the more successful you will be in life. Learn to plan and make decisions. These states will strengthen your desire to achieve your aim or purpose in life.

Learning to make decisions together is a very difficult mental adjustment. For some couples, it takes a long time to reach a decision when they consider something. It is true that people can make mistakes by making quick decisions, but actually, that doesn't matter, for even if a decision is wrong, people will learn from it and avoid repeating the mistake. It is good to allow yourself to make mistakes occasionally so that you learn to decide. A couple should learn how to decide and resolve questions together promptly, rather than postponing their decisions. Postponing decisions places a heavy burden on a person's mind. At some level the person keeps thinking about the choice and his or her mind becomes preoccupied and distracted.

I have noticed that many men who are judges or military officers are divorced by their wives. Their minds become preoccupied and burdened with the many decisions, choices, and alternatives they weigh each day and they become indecisive. When this pattern of preoccupation and mental distraction exists, people vacillate and sometimes cannot resolve even basic issues. When they want to sleep, rest, or enjoy time with their families, the unconscious mind reminds them, "You have left this issue unresolved; you haven't finished and resolved it; you must make the decision now." Then, the conscious mind pushes the question back, so that they again temporarily avoid dealing with it. But the person can't enjoy life. Their spouse sometimes feels that they are never really present in the home.

Prolonged indecision is such a powerful force that it can even cause sexual difficulties for a woman or a man later in life. When impotence occurs later in a man's life, it may not be the result of a physical difficulty, but of mental preoccupations or emotional issues. Many people don't understand that sexuality is influenced far more by mental factors than by physical virility. The mental and emotional aspects of sexuality dominate our lives. This is why understanding each other's minds and emotions is so important.

Men sometimes think that showing off their virility is the way for a husband to maintain or strengthen a marital relationship or establish deeper intimacy. Men may think that engaging in sex deepens their relationship with their wife, but a marriage cannot be established on the basis of a man's sexual virility—something more profound is needed. Sexuality and sexual skill alone are not an adequate basis for maintaining a life together. Genuine manhood is expressed in many other ways—by exhibiting consideration, caring, attentiveness, tolerance, patience, and generosity. Unfortunately, there is no place where the development of these qualities is taught, and our modern culture does not emphasize their value. A couple's parents, society, and the experiences of daily life help to remind them of the importance of these personal qualities, but ultimately, a couple learns through self-experimentation: two neophytes try to discover a path for themselves that allows them to create a loving life together.

Many marriages suffer from the problems of blame and accusations. A couple should be careful to control the tendency to become blaming or accusatory toward one another. Sometimes, people try to win arguments by making accusations to their spouse, "You have been unfaithful to me! I am faithful to you, but you are not sincere with me." These behaviors—blaming, making accusations, or calling your partner names—all damage a marriage. None of these behaviors builds a useful pattern of communication. It helps to develop the quality of forgiveness; human life is full of errors and mistakes, but everything, including our tendency toward criticism, can be controlled when love is at the center.

Change and growth inevitably occur over the course of a marriage, but criticism and blame never lead to change. Even death has no power to change people; the only factor that can really help anyone to change is love. If you have love, you can change anyone, or help anyone change and grow. However, you cannot be insincere and claim to genuinely love someone. These two factors—love and falsehood—cannot live together. In the process of loving, you become sincere, truthful, and selfless every way. As love grows and deepens between two people, these qualities are more fully understood.

Sometimes people disguise their selfishness or use spiritual practices as an excuse. Perhaps the husband has a headache and his wife thinks, "I want to practice my yoga; I'd rather do my headstand than take care of my husband." If a husband and wife want their love to grow, they should create the determination, "I want to do something for my spouse; I am prepared to do anything to give the best that I have for my partner." When a couple has such dedication and sincerity, then there will not be any misunderstandings between them.

The bridge of understanding between these two shores, between a man and a woman, should never be broken or damaged. She may hurt him, or he may hurt her, but neither should destroy or injure the bridge of understanding that they have been carefully building in their marriage over a long period of time. From the very beginning, there should be an agreement: "We will adjust ourselves to each other lovingly and never allow our relationship to be damaged, no matter what happens. We may disagree, but we will try to understand each other."

A mutual participation in some spiritual practice helps to increase understanding and bring spouses closer together. Some husbands allow their wives to go to church while they remain at home. In such situations the woman sometimes says, "I'm very fortunate that my husband wants me to do what I want, but I'm also sad because he never participates or shares this with me."

Sometimes a wife confuses the issue and expects her husband to follow her practices. Spouses must have respect for their partner, and not try to force or coerce the other to follow their path. It is best if two people discuss their goals, reach a decision, and then follow a path together. It is ideal if they learn to share spiritually. But don't force spiritual ideas on your spouse. Such rigid ideas have nothing to do with spirituality; they reflect egotism and power struggles. Give your partner time to find out for himself or herself what he or she believes as far as the path of spirituality is concerned.

In later life, if the partners do not share a spiritual conviction, a serious conflict may take place between married people. It seems that unless they have some shared conviction, partners can never come together with any real depth. If one wants to go to a particular church and the other does not, there may be a bad feeling between them. Real participation in marriage starts when both participate in a kind of spirituality that includes basic respect for each other's path, and also fosters love and understanding between them.

Meditation is a good way for couples to begin to deepen their understanding. Two people can begin to meditate together early in their marriage. Once their children are grown up and they have satisfied many of their material desires, then more of their time is free. They can turn their attention increasingly and more fully to spiritual matters. At this stage in life it is definitely helpful if they practice meditation, because the social and physical levels of union of marriage are not sufficient. A spiritual union should also grow, and it can develop and evolve through meditation.

When people begin to meditate they often find that, at first, it is somewhat difficult. Their mind remains preoccupied, and when the mind is in such a state, a person may sit down and go through the preliminaries, but not be able to meditate. However, two people can begin to help each other strengthen the habit of meditation by simply sitting together for a few minutes. Just as a couple relaxes together, works in the kitchen, shares their bed, and sits down together to watch TV, they can also learn to sit quietly together in meditation, sharing a state of stillness. A deep, wordless communication can be created without using the channels of speech or body language, which are more limited. Partners don't always need to rely upon speech, physical gestures or expressions to communicate, but can also learn to communicate love by living together in peaceful silence for a little time each day. When a husband and wife start to share their experiences in meditation they will continue to grow together.

If a person does not learn to adjust to his or her partner, that person can never really meditate deeply or attain universal consciousness or peace. If people try to meditate solely because they are disappointed or disillusioned with life or marriage, they will not achieve much. Do not use meditation to try to avoid the problems of life; meditation is only possible when the mind is free. When people learn to be joyful in their daily life, then meditation becomes deeper and more profound.

This process of nurturing a spiritual level of participation and communication is so important that if it is not present when old age comes, then the relationship usually weakens. It is important for couples to prepare for the experience of old age and learn to face together the issues of change, aging, and death. If the marital relationship is limited to being a physical relationship and has never grown beyond that, then the partners are not prepared for the challenges and questions of later life. Plant the seeds of spirituality early in your marriage so that they blossom in your old age. Then two people can live together joyfully and peacefully, attaining a shared spiritual height, and married life can become a serene way of living in the world.

No one can protect himself or herself from illness or death forever, but neither should a person live in the grasp of fear or dread, thinking, "I am afraid to lose my husband or wife because I am afraid of death. If he or she dies, who will look after me? What will happen to me?" There are people who live a long time, but with a constant sense of fear and worry; wondering what will happen if their partner divorces them or becomes ill. These fears arise because partners do not have a real spiritual connection and a sense of participation, and they prevent a healthy adjustment to life.

In India and other countries of the East, there was a tradition that couples would willingly separate after the age of fifty-five to pursue spiritual enlightenment. According to the custom, the husband would leave home and the grown-up children would look after their mother. In these traditional cultures, the adult children did not send their mother to a nursing home; she became the guardian of the children, the babysitter who imparted knowledge and love to her grandchildren. In these families, the husband left home and never returned, seeking spiritual enlightenment in a forest dwelling. In some parts of the world, that custom still exists.

There was another pattern in which couples did not separate. The wife might remind her husband of the purpose of their relationship by saying, "Where are you planning to go if you leave me? We had decided to live gether; let us enlighten ourselves together here." Th might have limited means, but they would live quie within those means, enjoying and sharing their spiritual tainment, and achieving a state of freedom from all fe;

and miseries before being separated by nature. Even facing death would not hurt or frighten them because they were enlightened. All their fears had dissolved because they had grown in wisdom and learned to see the purpose of their relationship clearly; they have made their relationship a means for attaining enlightenment.

As we become more spiritually evolved, we become less self-interested and self-involved; we should then also become more active in the world. We can continue to do our work and contribute to our world for as long as there is life. Life is meant to be an opportunity for selfless action, and we should always enjoy and find pleasure in these actions that we do for others.

All human beings enjoy doing pleasant things for themselves, but so do most animals. When a human being lives only on the primitive level—eating, sleeping, having sex, and experiencing fear because of the primitive urge for self-preservation—that person resembles an animal. The difference between animals and human beings is that people have the capacity to empathize, express compassion, and do things for the welfare of others, while most animals act to satisfy their own needs. Human beings have the power to continually increase their understanding of life, and as this understanding grows, they realize more completely how they are related to others. Finally, when their evolving awareness leads them to become totally selfless, they become free from the bondage of karma. Then, wise people experience a deep inner joy. They think, "This is life! What more do I need or desire? I need and want nothing else; when I desire nothing, then I am never disappointed in life."

We experience freedom and happiness when we have no sorrows or miseries. Try to eliminate all the possible sources of pain, physically, mentally, emotionally, and spiritually. Then happiness will gradually come. When a human being exhausts himself or herself by making a sincere effort, then grace dawns.

There was once a great sage called Karnava. This San-skrit name is very instructive and means, "One who cries like a baby." A baby cries for its mother's bosom and its mother may respond by offering the child a cookie or a doll, or another distraction. But if the baby goes on crying, the mother finally holds the infant to her bosom. Karnava cried because he could only be satisfied by the experience of enlightenment.

In a similar way, our mother nature has given us many external objects and pleasurable things to try to make us content. But if we are not satisfied with or placated by these small attractions, and if we have within us the flame that burns to attain the highest stage of happiness and consciousness, then we will eventually experience the Source, from which these simple attractions come. Like a child, we will finally be picked up and caressed by happi-ness itself.

Nature adjusts to us; nature helps us constantly. If we are weak and want to go on being weak, nature will re-inforce our weakness. We will have experiences that lead in that direction. On the other hand, if we really want to become stronger, then nature will help us to become stronger. Nature will provide challenges that help us grow spiritually.

We must learn to be strong from within. Genuine strength always comes from within ourselves and such strength is gentle because it comes from love. The more we do for others, the more we discover the secret of love. But the more selfish we become, the more we create boundaries and divisions between ourselves and others. The authentic sign of love is in giving, giving, and more giving—and in finding joy in that process of giving.

In the most ancient times of the Vedic period, there was no such thing as becoming a monk or a swami; two people would live together as man and wife and enlighten themselves. Others decided to live single lives and also became enlightened. For most people, it is better to live together and help each other by offering what you can for your partner without any ego involvement. The highest and finest expression of love is doing an action selflessly for your partner. Pray that you will experience that understanding.

The height of enlightenment is the realization that God is within ourselves. When we start to experience that reality, we enjoy life. Try to recognize God within each other. Then you will not be serving only your own wife or husband; you actually will be serving God in your thoughts, actions, and speech. When they achieve this relationship of love, respect, and awareness of the divine in each other, married people attain the highest state of enlightenment, even while they live in the world.

CHAPTER 6

Questions and Answers

Q: What is the biggest problem in the modern family?

A: The biggest problem in modern family life is that you do not know yourself! When you do not know yourself, you cannot communicate with others, even with your partner. Swami Rama Tirtha said, "Two people fight because they do not understand each other's language." He was not referring to the language we speak with the voice and tongue; he meant the mother of all languages, which is love.

If you have not experienced the deeper aspects of your own being then you do not really know what love is, no matter how long you have lived. If you do not fully know yourself, how can you communicate with others, especially the people with whom you live?

May you explore how to go within, to the deepest aspect of your being, the center of consciousness, from which consciousness flows in various degrees and grades. Learn how to experience that and how to be creative. When you know this serene, creative level of yourself, you become stronger. Then you can use your love, wisdom, and creativity to strengthen your family.

Q: How do we teach children to be creative?

A: Genuine creativity does not exist if a person is a good musician, dancer or painter, but is miserable in his or her emotional life. We don't need that kind of creativity! We need something truly creative, which helps us face the problems of daily living. And that truly creative resource is within ourselves.

Creativity is a natural, innate process—it will express itself automatically if children are loved, helped to feel secure, and allowed to be themselves. Allow your children's natural creativity to unfold in their own unique ways and don't attempt to influence children or force their personalities to develop according to your own preferences or expectations. Discover each child's unique way of being and support that—that is the surest way to help children become creative.

Q: How do we help children start on the right path, when there seem to be so many negative influences in our society?

A: Remind yourself of the power of your love and guidance, especially if you spend time with your children and provide them with a good example. Children always learn things through observing their parents. Set aside some time every day to be with them. Reassure yourself that genuine love and attention are the most important and powerful forces in a child's life.

I did not have parents, so I had only one example of this: my master. My master acted as both a mother and a father to me; he did everything for my welfare. If we have the zeal and willingness to sacrifice our time and personal

QUESTIONS AND ANSWERS   107

pleasures for the sake of our children, we can help children grow.

These days, some parents don't have time for their children. They provide canned, packaged foods, a borrowed education, broken homes, and the company of a babysitter. If this is how we express our love, then how can humanity survive? I think very seriously about this question.

Love is a language. Many people do not receive the "mother language" of love when they are children, so they remain wild. If someone is stern with you and then says, "I love you," you'll suddenly stop and listen to him or her. Love is the only power you can find that really helps in raising children.

Q: Why do we acquire so many negative attitudes and self-doubts? What can we do about them?

A: Everyone suffers as a result of the subtle suggestions and influences received from others. A wife suffers because her husband says, "You are disappointing, you are not beautiful, you are cross," and then the poor woman feels that she's bad. A mother tells her child, "You are bad, you are naughty, you are selfish." A father says, "You are bad, you are stupid, you are lazy." A teacher says, "This is a mistake; that is a mistake." No one tells us that there is goodness or strength within us. Because of such negative suggestions, which are a part of our experience and education in the world today, we forget our real self. We constantly identify ourselves with these negative suggestions, rather than with our strengths and potential. Then, we develop problems and self-doubts because of this identification with the suggestions of others.

Q: But how much do these suggestions really influence children?

A: Many parents make frequent, subtle suggestions to their children without realizing it. They influence children by their attitudes toward them, rather than teaching children to value themselves and think for themselves. Children often experience this at home. If their mothers and fathers are not wise and discriminate in their love or prefer one child to another, children develop problems.

The power of suggestion is hypnotic, and hypnosis is a large part of our modern education. That is a source of many people's suffering. If someone tells you that you are good then you feel flattered; if someone tells you that you are bad you feel crushed. Your self-attitude is dependent on the opinions of others.

There is an important difference between hypnosis and self-realization. You hypnotize yourself by taking in others' suggestions or judgments and then mentally repeating them, as when you say to yourself, "I'm not very good at this." Such self-suggestions make you feel weak and inadequate, because you forget your true nature. Throughout your life, you identify yourself with the negative suggestions and images you receive from others. On the path of self-realization, however, you set aside all these externally-based suggestions and directly experience your own nature. Through the process of meditation and increasing self-awareness, you begin to know yourself, rather than remaining dependent on the opinions of others.

Q: I love my wife very much, but I also feel very attached to the relationship. Are love and attachment the same?

A: Your love is a very positive force, but attachment is not helpful and will create misery for both of you. Attachment always brings pain, sooner or later. Your wife belongs to God, who has given her to you. Learn to love and serve her. If you cultivate the attitude of appreciating her as a gift, that's very helpful, but if you think, "She's mine," and expect her to satisfy your biological or emotional needs, then there is a problem with your attitude. If you think you do not have expectations, examine your reasons for becoming upset or angry; you will find that you expected something different from what took place. The test of your capacity to love is this: How much do you serve those you love, selflessly and without expectations?

Q: People all around the world unite as loving couples, and I wonder what the problem is—why do those relationships not remain loving?

A: A relationship between two people can remain loving, productive, and creative, provided that they understand the purpose of a relationship. A relationship is an opportunity to grow by expanding one's personality, becoming loving, unselfish, and sensitive to others. When you examine life, you realize that it is impossible to live without relationships. But instead of expanding, your ego often contracts and builds walls between yourself and those you claim to love—whether it is your spouse or your child. You need to recognize how the ego does this and seek to cultivate authentic selflessness, rather than the selfishness that seems so common in the modern world. Relationships can only remain loving if you expand your personality and do not let your ego create barriers and conflicts. Over time, people become angry and disappointed when their expectations of their partners are not met. They feel cheated because they expect another person to make them happy. Then they withdraw their love and create still more barriers with their anger. If we want a relationship to endure, we must continually forgive, accept, and let go of our unreasonable expectations.

Q: What is the practical difference between love and attachment? How do we become more loving and less attached?

A: People often say, "This is mine," or "that is mine," but what do we mean by the word, "mine" when we don't really know who we are? We say, "my wife" or "my children" and attempt to establish possessiveness or a sense of proprietorship over people. This is attachment; we want to control others. But our children and spouses do not belong to us; they exist to fulfill their own mission in life. We can only live together lovingly if we understand that people are meant for us to enjoy, but not to possess. Children are a gift to us but we cannot be attached to them, for they are not ours.

Attachment creates misery, but love makes us joyful. Love allows us to enjoy watching others grow, expand, and become independent. It brings us closer to wisdom, while attachment brings only pain. Attachment and love are opposites.

May you learn to love! That is your purpose on the earth—to learn to love people and to enlighten yourself. Through love you remain selfless, sharing and giving unconditionally. When you become attached you become selfish, expecting things from others and creating misery, bondage, and pain. Love is the force that creates wisdom and joy. Learn to love and resolve not to become attached. Then try to eliminate the attitude of possessiveness and expectation, whenever you become aware of it.

If you wish to eliminate your tendency to develop attachments, resolve not to let your ego become involved. Watch how your ego creates demands and expectations, all day long. This makes you weak and dependent. To live life skillfully you need to be strong, and this means to be free of attachments and expectations. Develop your inner strength, which is a capacity that all people have, and learn to use your inner strength with the help of your determination. Resolve to yourself, "No matter what happens, I will not become disturbed. I will maintain my equilibrium and tranquility when I am talking with people. When I deal with others, why am I disturbed? What do I expect from this person? Is this because I am weak?" If you constantly observe your progress, you will find that eventually you can recognize and eliminate your expectations. This means you become independent and loving, rather than attached.

Q: How do we help children to avoid using drugs?

A: There are criminals in this country—and everywhere in the world—introducing drugs to children. Why do you let such people be portrayed as heroes? Teach your children not to be swayed by those people. Children need to learn self-respect, self-confidence, and self-discipline. You can teach them this if you help them to first feel loved and accepted.

But children will only listen to you when you become an example to them. If you are not self-disciplined, then you will observe that children will not listen to you or respect you. Today, some children seem to be uncontrollable and unwilling to listen to their parents, because their parents lie to them, fail to love them, and are selfish. If you want to help your children avoid drugs, then learn to love your children and help them become strong. For a few minutes every day, sit quietly in meditation; learn to go within, love others, and establish peace within yourself. Then you can give your children love and acceptance. When parents teach children to appreciate themselves and find strength and self-confidence within, they can easily help them avoid using drugs.

Q: Should children be disciplined? If so, how?

A. Of course! But first the parents should be *self*-disciplined! Children need to be taught how to behave and how not to behave, and it is very challenging for a parent to do this without suppressing the child's individuality. It takes time to discipline wisely, because you cannot force a child or act from your own frustrations and impatience.

The first, tender years of a child's life—until the child is five to seven—are the most important time. During that time, especially, parents should never be harsh or rigid with the child. Learn to provide unconditional love and try to direct the child's attention and activity in helpful, constructive ways. This requires time and awareness on the parents' part.

Physical force or violence should never be used on children. If you do not want your children to hit or strike others, why should you strike or slap them? Violence means that you have no self-discipline or self-control; gentle, loving attention is best. Children will accept your guidance when they know that you love them.

As children become older, they need more firmness and a different type of discipline. At this stage they should not be encouraged to remain dependent but helped to become strong and self-confident. The discipline needed by older children includes a daily schedule with regular bedtime hours, and a good, well-balanced diet so that they learn the value of self-control. It is easy to lose one's temper and shout at children, but it is better to talk to children and help them understand why certain behaviors are wrong. Parents should also listen to their children, and respect their ideas, opinions, and attitudes. If parents listen attentively to their children, they will find that their children actually teach them how to become better parents. A child's behavior will show you where you are making mistakes or where you need to improve yourself. Giving children the love and attention they need is far more important than any other task—it is the process of becoming their first spiritual teachers.

Q: Please explain what you mean by the phrase, "using the force of your own personality on a child."

A: You adults do not understand how much your children want your love and attention! Adults often try to mold children to meet their expectations or fulfill their own desires. When you do this, by giving praise or attention for fulfilling your personal ego desires, you are using force on a subtle but powerful level. Sometimes children have nightmares because of their sensitivity to this pressure.

For example, when you ask your child to remember and recite a poem or to behave in some way, it may be because you want to show off to others how wonderful your child is or how wonderful you are. So your child sings a sweet poem, "Twinkle, twinkle, little star," and dances. The child wants to live according to your desires. The child wants your approval and love, but you are unknowingly imposing your personality on your child, for your own ego gratification. Then, at night, the child sings the same song in a dream, because there was some feeling of pressure or conflict. And you say, "My child was dreaming, 'Twinkle, twinkle, little star,' " and you think that this is funny or charming, but that is not a good sign. The poor child's sleep was disturbed because of the pressure you created. A sensitive and wise parent avoids creating conflict or pressure in a child to perform according to the parent's own ego needs.

Q: How exactly does one learn to love?

A: Love means appreciating and enjoying the divine essence in another person. But how do we do this? There are two aspects to love: first, we seek to eliminate any tendency that negates love. And second, we seek to create an awareness of the perfection within the other. The *Yoga Sutras* give a definition of love, teaching that the first goal of love is *ahimsa* or "non-harming." This means we seek to avoid harming, injuring or hurting those we love, either physically or mentally. If we harm or injure another person, then that is not love. If we always do that which is best for those we love, then we love them sincerely.

After you have achieved the capacity to avoid harming others, then the next step is to learn to feel real joy and delight in serving others. I'll give you an example of this that once amazed me. Many years ago, in Calcutta, during the time when there was alien rule in India, there was an artificial food shortage created by the government. There were simply no food supplies. Two people were fighting—a young man and an old man—and it was an intense verbal battle. The police stopped them and asked why they were fighting.

The young man said, "There is only one loaf of bread; I want this old man to eat it because he may only live for a few days."

And the old man said, "I am dying; why are you worried about me? You are young; you need to eat!"

And the police did not know how to react in that case! Finally the old man said, "Son, you have to live for the good of the country. Please eat! I want you to enjoy this and I'll be delighted if you eat it."

When you learn to love others, you learn to give, and there are no conditions or limitations to that. You give unconditionally, without any reservation. Love is one of the few human qualities that can lead you to a glimpse of the divine, if you develop that capacity fully. Then a higher knowledge is revealed, rolling down from the infinite library within you. When this occurs, you'll find that a higher force begins to guide you in many of your decisions.

Q: Should we really focus so much on our own families— shouldn't we strive to love all people?

A: It is good to have the goal of universal love, but first, you should learn to love in a practical way those who are closest to you. Learn to love and accept others, instead of striving or expecting. The problem is that people begin to expect love from others, and everyone expects so much! That is attachment, rather than love. Love means giving. Give all that you can, with your mind, action, and speech, to your beloved or to the people whom you love, without any expectations. What good is it to love humanity as an abstraction, when you cannot live in peace with one man or one woman? Family life is the arena for your first lessons with love. Then, as you develop your capacity to love, expand your love from your family to your community, and eventually to the whole world.

Q: How can we improve our marriages and families?

A: If it is difficult for you to accept *yourself*, how will you accept me? How can you appreciate and value your own people? If you do not have the willingness to learn to understand and accept others—your spouse, children, and family—then don't be a hypocrite; don't get married!

Learn to love and accept yourself first. The goal is to love and appreciate the finest aspect of yourself, which is not the body or the breath alone, but the individual soul, the source of consciousness within. Once you have learned to love your soul, you'll find that all souls are one and the same—the Self of all is within you. As you become increasingly conscious of that reality, then your family life will be transformed.

Q: How can I help a child who seems to make mistakes almost all the time, such as stumbling and dropping things?

A: If a child stumbles and makes frequent mistakes, the first step is to take the child by the hand and demonstrate the correct behavior to him. Then, when it is safe, let the child walk or do the activity by himself, according to his capacity. You should thoughtfully observe the child and try to understand whether the child stumbles or make mistakes because he is trying to go beyond his capacity or is not strong enough to walk alone. Perhaps the child is not paying attention or is emotionally upset, and those emotions are interfering with his concentration. If you understand the main reasons why a child makes mistakes, then you can help him. Every child can learn if he or she is given guidance and taught to pay attention. Don't allow a child to continue to make mistakes without helping him. It is not good for a child's self-esteem to make mistakes and constantly feel frustrated. Help children solve their problems and understand what the difficulties are.

Q: What would you do to help a child who is five years old and very wild and hard to control?

A: Observe the child and determine why the child behaves wildly. Is the child eating foods that agitate his nervous system and make it hard for him to control himself? Is the child frequently overtired or emotionally upset? If so, why? Perhaps the child is very frightened or angry about something that has happened to him. If you want to help a child who has such difficulties, you first need to become a good observer and try to understand the child.

Actually, the emotional problems people experience are never related to themselves alone. When a person has a problem, the person has some relationship in their life that is causing difficulties. It may be a relationship with a person or it may be a sense of connection with some object about which there is a conflict. Every emotion that a person has is related to some other person or object. Life and relationships are essentially one and the same; if you have a relationship, you will have emotions.

Many people try to help children with their emotions without discovering in which relationship there is a problem. The difficulty may lie in a relationship with the parents, teacher, siblings, or friends, or it may be a problem with someone who dislikes the child at school or in the neighborhood. The moment a person creates animosity towards another, they become related. An enemy is simply someone with whom you have a negative relationship. Try to determine the source of the problem. If you discover what the underlying problem is, then you can help a child become free.

Q: Should children be taught to meditate?

A: When children understand the value of meditation, then introduce the practice, if they are interested. Help them learn if that is their goal. It is not a good idea to impose your interest in meditation on your children, however. If you impose meditation or any practice on children, they will resent it and it will create a conflict for them. If young children observe their parents meditating early in their life, they naturally develop an interest in meditation. Young children are eager to imitate adults and experiment with new behaviors. Later, when they are older, if children learn why meditation is good for them and begin to enjoy the experience of sitting in meditation for brief periods, they will continue the practice.

When a child wants to learn to meditate, first teach the child to sit quietly and be still for a few minutes. Mothers are actually the first teachers in the practice of meditation and concentration, because when children are young, they will follow their mother's example.

Q: Are there more healthy, spiritual families in the East or the West?

A: Spirituality is not the property of any particular country or region, so please don't think that all the people, animals, fish, and birds in the East are enlightened! Sometimes people idealize the East and travel there, coming back disappointed. Spirituality is something individual; wherever you live, once you become aware of your inner nature and understand your full potential, then you become spiritual.

Yes, there are some strong traditions in the East. In these family traditions they don't teach their children from books or lectures alone, but instead, children learn by following their parents' examples—seeing how parents act, talk, and practice. Children learn mostly by example.

There are certain facilities in the West that are also very helpful—there is abundant food, and clean spacious homes, and people have many of the necessities of life, but the West has become materialistic and now the East is following in this direction. We don't want to live for a hundred years like foolish, talking animals, do we? What good are a long life and material comfort if you do not know why you want to live?

Spirituality and prosperity are two different qualities. This is one difference that you'll notice between the East and West. There has traditionally been a value system in the East that does not seem to be found as often in the Western hemisphere, although there is also spirituality in the West. Generally, however, the West seeks an external glamour and external achievements. Its values are still there, but in the main culture, you are slowly losing ground.

In fifty years' time you have lost much that has value. Fifty years ago, for example, many Jewish and Catholic homes had strong, loving families. Today you still find homes where the family follows a discipline, and such families are beautiful. But why does the West have a fifty percent divorce rate? This is because you no longer follow your own traditions or disciplines.

Spirituality is the same, East or West. Wherever we live, we can only make progress by becoming spiritually aware. Without this experience, we can never know the finest aspect of ourselves. That attainment is our birthright—to grow and to attain the height of spiritual awareness, in which we learn to love all and exclude none.

Q: What does it mean to teach children to live a successful life?

A: You send your children to good schools so that they will become successful on the material level in life. On this level, success means that they earn enough to live comfortably. Yet, unfortunately, you don't train your children to be peaceful, calm, healthy, and energetic, or to know their inner nature.

Thus, this deeper facet of life is missing. Children need an integrated education, rather than a one-sided education that emphasizes only material success. In the modern society, something is missing somewhere; that is why none of you is truly healthy; you suffer from a variety of physical and emotional diseases.

After you receive your education in the colleges and universities, you must complete your real education, or else your college degree can not help you very much. In the modern world, you need to answer an important question: how can you live in health, peace, and serenity? Learn to establish a balance between the world within and the world around you, rather than learning to function only in the external world. A few minutes of meditation every day can help you become free from the external stresses that you experience. This will help you to achieve a deeper awareness of yourself, as well as to achieve success on the material level.

Q: Recently there have been many popular books on the "inner child," which suggest the idea that there is an inner child that may have been hurt in our childhood. What is the difference between the soul and the inner child? Is the soul the same as the "inner child?"

A: The soul is that which is beyond mind and personality; it is your essential nature. The soul does not need therapy or training, for it is always free. The soul does not need to be cured or healed; it seeks only to be experienced and known. This knowledge brings great peace and joy.

When you talk of the "inner child," you are talking about an aspect of your mind and personality. The human personality always has limits and conflicts—it needs to be improved and balanced. You have to train your mind like you train a child—with love. The ancient sages learned to train the mind using a variety of methods. The "inner child" is your mind and emotions, which you must learn to train with love. Many of the practices of meditation and yoga help to heal and train the personality, but the ultimate goal is to go beyond, and experience the soul or essence.

Q: How can meditation improve a relationship?

A: Many people think it's difficult to achieve peace in a marriage, but actually it's not hard! The challenge is to learn to create peace within yourself, and then it is possible to understand your spouse and create peace together. The best way to establish peace with your husband or wife—as well as peace in society—is to know yourself, using the method of meditation.

Everyone learns to move and function in the external world, but no one teaches you how to find peace within yourself. In meditation, you learn to understand yourself on all levels. It is very simple and easy to meditate. You don't need to disturb other family members or neglect your duties. You simply sit in meditation at exactly the same time every day.

Many people have difficulties in their relationships because they have not learned to establish a balance in their own minds—there is no tranquility within. The first goal for a happy married life is to learn to compose yourself; learn to be strong and serene from within. Then it is easy to live lovingly with others.

Q: Please comment on the changing roles of mothers and fathers in the modern world.

A: Traditionally, mothers are the founders of the family system—they nurture this aspect of life and impart the first steps of education to children. They provide love and acceptance. This is a very important role because it is the first step in the child's spiritual life, and playing this part is a great sacrifice for a modern mother.

If a man works outside the home, he becomes the provider; these days, many women work outside the home and become providers, too. Still, the mother has a more important role than a man, especially in a child's early life. This is a very important time because a child is very aware of and sensitive to, the surrounding environment during this early period. Providing a safe, loving environment establishes a foundation for a child's life.

The role of the father is important, too, especially as children leave infancy. Fathers help children to expand and learn through their love and attention. However, sometimes husbands are also like children. When husbands neglect their responsibilities and become like children, it becomes very difficult for a woman to manage a family. In the modern world, some men have become irresponsible. They may become "workaholics" and ignore the responsibilities of helping to raise the children, or they may abandon their children and families. It creates great problems in society when men abandon these duties, and there are many children whose lives are damaged by it. All over the world, thousands of children are abandoned and it becomes impossible for them to learn to be good citizens or healthy people.

What our society needs today is men and women who realize the importance of creating healthy families. It is helpful for women to develop themselves on all levels— physically, emotionally, intellectually, and spiritually, rather than merely imitating men and competing with them. The only place where modern women are wrong is that they have entered into a competition with man. If modern men become unbalanced, aggressive, agitated, and stressed, women become agitated and stressed. If men are crude, nasty, and vulgar, women also become rude, nasty and vulgar. What happens in this process is that women are not using their own power and brilliance. They are imitating someone else in their external behavior and identifying themselves with men, accepting their shallow values, which causes problems.

In some ways, woman has a greater capacity than man. For example, often a woman can tolerate more pain than a man, as when a woman gives birth. The capacity of woman is immense. Man has a brute, external force and is more active than woman in many ways, but actually, woman has more inner power.

If there is ever to be any transformation in the world, it will not come from men. Men's resources are exhausted, as far as creating a peaceful home or world is concerned. Men can never establish peace without the help of women. But women should not imitate men or accept their values.

Women can do a lot in the modern world to improve social conditions. You can create a better future for your children; you can do wonders to heal and transform society—if you understand your own worth. But if you are looking toward men for answers, you are mistaken: man is disturbed and confused. He can create technology but he cannot do anything to truly help the world. Nothing profound can be achieved using the resources of men alone. The answers are within your own families.

Homes should be centers from which peace radiates, but in today's society, it is rare to find homes that fulfill this potential. If your homes are disturbed, where will human beings find peace? Will you find peace at your office? By eating a hamburger? By eating Kentucky Fried Chicken? These are not superficial questions: Where will you find peace if you do not learn to create it in your homes?

Genuine peace dwells in loving homes and it should never be disturbed or disrupted. A wise person never disturbs his or her home, because it is the center of the community and the world. But if you lack a center, what will happen to you? How will children learn to become human beings rather than talking animals? In the noise of the external world, a home should be a refuge—a center of peace and comfort. May you create peace in your homes!

There is also another center within you that should remain at peace. Do a simple experiment: meditate so that you are relaxed and calm, and then let your spouse or child become angry. If you are relaxed and composed, you will not feel so impatient or upset; you can handle things without becoming angry. If you lose your inner balance and serenity, life becomes a battle.

Modern women have experienced discrimination in their jobs and work, so they feel insecure and fear being seen as inferior. Women are not inferior; let all women and men value and appreciate a finer and more powerful role—the subtle work of creating love and a healthy society. This role should be appreciated by both men and women. Throughout history, the power of love has given hope to humanity, and unless you realize the importance of this power within your own mind, the external world will remain distorted.

If you forget that you are creators, your homes will crumble, and if the homes crumble, the lives of children will be destroyed. Women who are mothers have more responsibility than any other person, and that responsibility should be enjoyed, rather than carried as a burden. Woman has played a great role in the history of humanity, but man has not understood woman, and that's why he suffers. Man creates and accepts his own suffering. He has no time for life! He's so involved with superficial, external things—he's so busy that he gets lost in the external world.

If a mother remains at home, particularly when her children are very young, she plays an important and powerful role in caring for her children. But in the modern world, people have not yet fully appreciated the importance of this role in the first stage of the development of a human being, and society has not accepted its responsibility to support this process. It is important that children receive love, attention, and support. Women have the love to do that; woman is a symbol of love. This is not flattery; I'm telling you the truth.

Q: How can we improve the education of children?

A: There's a serious limitation in our educational system, because children are not taught to be aware of and examine things in the world within themselves. They remain strangers to themselves, but they expect their relationships to be perfect. They expect to be able to communicate with others, yet they cannot communicate with themselves. It's important for children to understand the value of life, with its currents and cross-currents, and thus value their own individual growth.

Human beings have tremendous potential, provided they are taught to train themselves on all levels—physically, mentally and spiritually. But the only strength a person can rely on is inner strength, and that inner strength is based on love. How do children learn inner strength, love, and awareness in the modern world? If they do not learn these capacities in the educational system or in their families, they have only received half an education. As adults, we should take responsibility for our society. Let us live for the whole human family; let us live with respect and love for all creatures, and let us teach children how to become aware of themselves on all levels.

Q: How can women help to change the world?

A: Man has been very selfish and cruel all over the world; it's a pity that man has not given equal opportunity and equal rights to woman. I don't believe in extremes, but I think women should have their rights. Why should a man think he is superior to woman or why should a woman think she is superior to man? Men and women are equal partners.

The modern world has ceased to respect women, and women have been exploited all over the world. I was shocked when I heard that there were movies made in South America where actresses were killed. Human life was destroyed! What kind of insanity is this? Everywhere you go, there are posters of products and a half-nude woman is posing with them. I'm saddened by the vulgar pattern of exploiting women. In the modern culture this is considered to be acceptable. Women should be respected, revered, and loved. I think the time has come when both women and men are becoming aware of this.

Woman is the creator of our society and of the entire world that we see around us. The first architect of society is woman. When woman became pregnant she wanted a shelter, a safe place to raise her child, and she wanted man to help her. The nature of this motivation is to love and care for others. In this capacity, a woman is definitely superior to man, because by nature, man does not think first of the welfare of others.

I am referring to those women who are genuine women, aware of the purpose of life, not those who are selfish or irresponsible or who have lost their own values. If there is any force that can change the course of humanity, it is woman. When we understand that the responsibility for children's development and education should be given to women, there will be dramatic changes in how we manage our culture.

Q: Is it wrong to end a relationship? What if there is never any peace or harmony in a relationship, no matter what you do to try to improve it?

A: A human being cannot live without relationships, and if a relationship fails, a person wants to replace what he loses with something or someone else. By changing the object or person, a person does not stop having relationships. But a relationship can become like a habit, and the more dependency there is in the relationship, the less enjoyment. Then people become angry and want to leave.

Some people have relationships merely for the sake of their personal enjoyment. They think that they will find pleasure here and there, so they constantly seek new relationships to fulfill their selfish desires. That's a complete disaster! Learn to enjoy the relationships that you have, instead of searching for new relationships, becoming increasingly more distracted and miserable in the process.

Sometimes, however, you experience a negative, destructive relationship because the person you chose was not healthy or good for you. If this is the case, you should either work to change the relationship or leave it. You will need to be aware of whether you are being sincere and honest with yourself in this matter.

Q: My husband loses his temper and shouts all the time, and I don't know what to do.

A: When he begins to get upset, decide that you will remain quiet and observe him, and after a few minutes when he quiets down, you can calmly ask him why he is so upset and why he is saying such irrational things. Then he will probably apologize.

In any relationship, it is helpful if both people agree that if either person is emotionally upset, the other will not reply emotionally. If someone upsets you emotionally, it means that you are weaker than that person. Often modern women and men use this tactic on each other: "I have power! I can upset this person emotionally!" People know what things will make you upset and sometimes they will use that to torture you, if you let them.

Learn not to allow anyone to hurt you, and also learn not to hurt others. This becomes possible when you learn how to guide your emotions. Your emotions can be chan-

nelled in a creative way, rather than being expressed nega-
tively. All emotions are related to something in the external world; as a human being, deep within, you are perfect
and complete.

Q: How do we make progress in developing our society?

A: When we examine what we call progress in the western hemisphere and observe how the sciences have pro-
gressed, we notice certain things. Those who have studied
medicine and health know that in the modern world, even
though many diseases have been eliminated, people still
suffer from other diseases that are not entirely curable by
medicine alone—they are diseases of stress and the modern lifestyle. We human beings should learn to come back
to our inner "home," take responsibility for ourselves, and
create a holistic, healthy approach to life.

We need a type of training program in our homes
through which we train ourselves to remain healthy and
balanced. If we accomplish this our training programs will
be accepted by children, and children will follow a pattern
of healthy living. Many human problems occur due to a
lack of self-discipline, and we can solve many of these
problems, including alcohol and drug abuse, violence and
crime, if we introduce a program of self-awareness and
self-discipline, not in the colleges and universities, but in
the homes.

Children often behave badly because the adults around
them are not doing what is right. Children learn from
adults and imitate the things they observe; then adults
blame children for their behavior. Please become examples so that children will follow your guidance—become
examples of love, non-violence, and selfless service to your
communities and to the world. In homes where the parents serve as examples, children behave well. They are self-
confident, they respect others, and they learn to discipline
themselves. In the modern society, however, the training

ground for human beings is crumbling, because there are few parents able to become examples. Few parents teach their children how to love, share, and be truthful because they themselves do not know how.

Children observe how we live, what we value, and whom we admire. They see the difference between what we say and what we do. We know the language, the words, and the principles, but we do not know how to execute them and carry them into our daily life. As long as a practical training in the home is missing, we will continue to lack something. We adults are hurting ourselves and we are also hurting the children.

If there is ever to be any meaningful, peaceful, constructive change in the world, it will take place from the family unit. When people learn to love others and respect life, they will not create violence in the streets, hurting others and destroying things. That peaceful evolution will begin from the foundation of loving homes. The center of a home is parents' love for each other and for their children.

We can create good homes and healthy children. Once we achieve this, we can change the whole world. Then, we can create another step in the evolution of civilization. If we decide today that we really want to create a peaceful society, and if we resolve to change our present way of life, we have the power to transform the world in thirty or forty years. It is a question of deciding the direction that we want to go. We have done enough research on material sciences and material success. We must change ourselves and our habits, so that we can raise healthy children who learn to love and serve others. This is possible!

About the Author

BORN IN 1925 in northern India, Swami Rama was raised from early childhood by a great Bengali yogi and saint who lived in the foothills of the Himalayas. In his youth he practiced the various disciplines of yoga science and philosophy in the traditional monasteries of the Himalayas and studied with many spiritual adepts, including Mahatma Gandhi, Sri Aurobindo, and Rabindranath Tagore. He also traveled to Tibet to study with his grandmaster.

He received his higher education at Bangalore, Prayaga, Varanasi, and Oxford University, England. At the age of twenty-four he became Shankaracharya of Karvirpitham in South India, the highest spiritual position in India. During this term he had a tremendous impact on the spiritual customs of that time: he dispensed with useless formalities and rituals, made it possible for all segments of society to worship in the temples, and encouraged the instruction of women in meditation. He renounced the dignity and prestige of this high office in 1952 to return to the Himalayas to intensify his yogic practices.

After completing an intense meditative practice in the cave monasteries, he emerged with the determination to serve humanity, particularly to bring the teachings of the East to the West. With the encouragement of his master, Swami Rama began his task by studying Western philosophy and psychology. He worked as a medical consultant in London and assisted in parapsychological research in Moscow. He then returned to India, where he established an ashram in Rishikesh. He completed his degree in homeopathy at the medical college in Darbhanga in 1960. He came to the United States in 1969, bringing his knowledge and wisdom to the West. His teachings combine Eastern spirituality with modern Western therapies.

Swami Rama was a freethinker, guided by his direct experience and inner wisdom, and he encouraged his students to be guided in the same way. He often told them, "I am a messenger, delivering the wisdom of the Himalayan sages of my tradition. My job is to introduce you to the teacher within."

Swami Rama came to America upon the invitation of Dr. Elmer Green of the Menninger Foundation of Topeka, Kansas, as a consultant in a research project investigating the voluntary control of involuntary states. He participated in experiments that helped to revolutionize scientific thinking about the relationship between body and mind, amazing scientists by his demonstrating, under laboratory conditions, precise conscious control of autonomic physical responses and mental functioning, feats previously thought to be impossible.

Swami Rama founded the Himalayan International Institute of Yoga Science and Philosophy, the Himalayan Institute Hospital Trust in India, and many centers throughout the world. He is the author of numerous books on health, meditation, and the yogic scriptures. Swami Rama left his body in November 1996.

The Himalayan Institute

FOUNDED IN 1971 by Swami Rama, the Himalayan Institute has been dedicated to helping people grow physically, mentally, and spiritually by combining the best knowledge of both the East and the West.

Our international headquarters is located on a beautiful 400-acre campus in the rolling hills of the Pocono Mountains of northeastern Pennsylvania. The atmosphere here is one to foster growth, increased inner awareness, and calm. Our grounds provide a wonderfully peaceful and healthy setting for our seminars and extended programs. Students from around the world join us here to attend programs in such diverse areas as hatha yoga, meditation, stress reduction, Ayurveda, nutrition, Eastern philosophy, psychology, and other subjects. Whether the programs are for weekend meditation retreats, week-long seminars on spirituality, months-long residential programs, or holistic health services, the attempt here is to provide an environment of gentle inner progress. We invite you to join with us in the ongoing process of personal growth and development.

The Institute is a nonprofit organization. Your membership in the Institute helps to support its programs. Please call or write for information on becoming a member.

Institute Programs, Services, and Facilities

Institute programs share an emphasis on conscious holistic living and personal self-development, including:

Special weekend or extended seminars to teach skills and techniques for increasing your ability to be healthy and enjoy life

Meditation retreats and advanced meditation and philosophical instruction

Vegetarian cooking and nutritional training

Hatha yoga and exercise workshops

Residential programs for self-development

Holistic health services and Ayurvedic Rejuvenation Programs through the Institute's Center for Health and Healing.

The Institute's *Quarterly Guide to Programs and Other Offerings* is free within the USA. To request a copy, or for further information, call 800-822-4547 or 570-253-5551, fax 570-253-9078, e-mail bqinfo@himalayaninstitute.org, or write the Himalayan Institute, /RR 1, Box 400, /Honesdale, PA 18431-9706 USA, or visit our Web site at www.himalayaninstitute.org.

The Himalayan Institute Press

The Himalayan Institute Press has long been regarded as "The Resource for Holistic Living." We publish dozens of titles, as well as audio and video tapes, that offer practical methods for harmonious living and inner balance. Our approach addresses the whole person—body, mind, and spirit—integrating the latest scientific knowledge with ancient healing and self-development techniques.

As such, we offer a wide array of titles on physical and psychological health and well-being, spiritual growth through meditation and other yogic practices, and the means to stay inspired through reading sacred scriptures and ancient philosophical teachings.

Our sidelines include the Japa Kit for meditation practice, The Neti™Pot, the ideal tool for sinus and allergy sufferers, and The Breath Pillow,™ a unique tool for learning health-supportive breathing—the diaphragmatic breath.

Subscriptions are available to a bimonthly magazine, *Yoga International,* which offers thought-provoking articles on all aspects of meditation and yoga, including yoga's sister science, Ayurveda.

For a free catalog call 800-822-4547 or 570-253-5551, e-mail: hibooks@himalayaninstitute.org, fax 570-251-7812, or write the Himalayan Institute Press, RR 1, Box 405, Honesdale, PA 18431-9709, USA, or visit our Web site at www.himalayaninstitute.org.